INTELLIGENCE UNCHAINED

Skilligence®:
The Framework for Building
Learning Ability Throughout Your Life

Career • Relationships • Self

By Menko Rose
PhC, MS, LMFT (retired)
with Sally Rose

www.skilligenceworkshops.com

Copyright © 2019 by Menko Rose

All rights reserved. This book is licensed to the original purchaser only. In accordance with the U.S. Copyright Act of 1976, the scanning, uploading, and electronic sharing of any part of this book without the permission of the author is unlawful piracy and theft of the author's intellectual property. Duplication or distribution via any means is illegal and a violation of international copyright law, subject to criminal prosecution and upon conviction, fines, and/or imprisonment.

Any eBook format cannot be legally loaned or given to others. No part of this book may be reproduced or transmitted in any form or by any means, electronic or mechanical, including photocopying, recording, or by any information storage and retrieval system, without the written permission of the Publisher, except where permitted by law.

If you would like to use material from the book (other than for review purposes), prior written permission must be obtained by e-mail to skilligence@comcast.net. Thank you for your support of author's rights.

First Publication July 2019 v. 1.0
Printed in the USA

ISBN-13: 978-1-948883-07-8

Table of Contents

CHAPTER ONE 1
    INTRODUCTION

CHAPTER TWO 12
    SKILL 1: RELAXATION

CHAPTER THREE 26
    SKILL 2: ATTENTION

CHAPTER FOUR 35
    SKILL 3: MOTIVATION

CHAPTER FIVE 54
    SKILL 4: MEMORY

CHAPTER SIX 66
    SKILL 5: COMMUNICATIONS

CHAPTER SEVEN 81
    SKILL 6: COMPUTATIONS

CHAPTER EIGHT 100
    SKILL 7: CONCEPT FORMATION

CHAPTER NINE 116
    SKILL 8: PROBLEM SOLVING

CHAPTER TEN 134
    SKILL 9: CREATIVITY

CHAPTER ELEVEN 153
    SKILL 10: PRECISION LEARNING

CHAPTER TWELVE 167
    IMPLEMENTATION

CHAPTER THIRTEEN 174
    SUMMARY: THE BOOK IN A NUTSHELL

CHAPTER ONE

INTRODUCTION

Having experienced war, my thing is peace.
I believe that, as more of us develop higher intelligence, the chances for achieving global peace grows.

I believe that, sooner or later, if we don't create a secure structure for a peaceful world, our luck will run out — some crazy jerk will start a nuclear war and we humans, and most other animals and plants, will be no more.

That is why I developed Skilligence.

Skilligence is based on the idea that intelligence is improvable. The Skilligence Framework is designed to help individuals improve their intelligence — and most anyone can use it.

Historically, individuals' intelligence, their ability to learn, generally stabilized as they matured. The resulting habitual, predictable behavior benefitted the society, the family and the individual.

Yet over the ages, the circumstances in which we exist have evolved. The need for higher levels of intelligence has grown, and lately it has grown at an accelerating rate. Now, all three — society, family and individuals — tend to benefit as individuals expand their ability and their motivation to learn.

Fortunately, recent academic research has illuminated the dynamics of the learning process. Now, that process is readily converted into a skill. The Skilligence system harnesses this research to enable you to convert your intelligence into an improvable skill.

I believe that the principles behind Skilligence can help individuals enhance their lives, deriving more enjoyment from their family life, their work and their communities. For example, it's an ideal tool to help veterans gain skills and adapt to civilian life. In a free society, the higher a person's intelligence, the more likely he or she is to cope well with his or her life — to acquire competence, gain satisfaction, security and an increasing degree of financial freedom and happiness.

Human intelligence — that is, our ability to learn — is our most valuable single possession. It allows us to succeed at what we treasure most, including in love, parenting, careers, hobbies and friendship.

Even a slightly higher intelligence would allow many of us to budget better, parent better, work better, be better spouses and, in general, enjoy ourselves more. Perhaps most significantly, it would enable us to acquire the knowledge and skills required to take pleasure in and prosper at a more satisfying and better-paying career.

Virtually anyone can improve his or her intelligence. And, often, even a slight increase in one of its components will trigger a large increase in overall intelligence.

The evolution of intelligence
To understand how improvable intelligence is, it's helpful to also understand how it has evolved.

Human intelligence evolved slowly at first over many millions of years, and then, more recently, at an accelerating rate. Initially, its evolution depended upon the simultaneous evolution of the brain and of the hand and thumb, along with the tongue and lips and vocal chords.

These critical changes have allowed humans to use tools and to communicate, to work and to create together.

And — we're not done evolving.

The world's societies are becoming more and more complex. Their individual human members, therefore, require increasing levels of learning ability in order to survive and thrive. Fortunately, at the same time, the academic community is providing individuals with a growing understanding of intelligence, one that enables those who are interested, and willing, to raise their learning ability to match society's new needs.

Which is what this publication is about — a set of tools to use to improve your intelligence, your overall learning ability.

THE EVOLUTION OF SKILLIGENCE

The early years
Before we dive into the components of an improving intelligence, here is a little of my background, my evolution, and how Skilligence came to be.

I came upon this understanding of the huge improvability of intelligence quite by accident.

During World War II, I suffered two head injuries. The first occurred during infantry training at Camp Van Dorn in Mississippi, when five of my front teeth were shattered by shrapnel from a hand grenade. It was the summer of 1944, and I was in a coma for nearly two months.

The second time, in Luxembourg during the Battle of the Bulge, I was thrown, arcing through the air some 25 yards, from the explosion of a howitzer shell. As I lay on the ground unconscious, my squad members presumed I was dead.

It was 7 January 1945. Thankfully, I was out for only a couple of minutes.

And, luckily, though they were pretty sure I was done-for, two members of my squad came back to check on me. One kicked me and I must have stirred, for they leaned down, grabbed me under my shoulders, stood me up and walked me until I was able to walk on my own.

Had they listened to the first soldier's report that I was dead, and left me there in the ice and snow, I surely would have frozen to death, and quickly — it was one of the coldest winters on record.

As luck and war would have it, I took shrapnel again later in the day, in my knee. And it got worse. As the day wore on, all but one of the members of my squad were either killed or badly wounded. Most were killed.

After that, I was sent back to England for a couple of months of rest and rehabilitation, for both my injuries and for frostbite in my hands and feet. Interestingly, I was mute during most of my rehabilitation and often still find communicating difficult. To this day I don't know why, but I've always assumed the explosions caused damage to my brain and communication processes, but some of it may have been from intense fear.

Back stateside, in spring of 1946, I returned to Cornell University, where I'd been studying before entering the Army. I majored in economics, minored in philosophy and completed a pre-med program, graduating in the spring of 1948. I was highly motivated but, at that time, lowly capable. It was frustrating. My GPA was 2.09, barely above failing.

After graduation, I followed my father onto Wall Street, embarking on a career in finance, first in a series of clerk positions, then as a customers' broker and then as a securities analyst. Interestingly, I scored the highest ever at that time on the stock exchange test for customers broker.

Yet, by 1951, I had been fired from my last three jobs. All within three years, 1948 to 1951.

At the time, it felt all bad to me.

In retrospect I realize it wasn't. It wasn't all due to my failings. In fact, right after the last one, I received two offers of jobs at two different companies with better reputations than the ones I had been with, and perhaps better suited to me.

But that didn't register with me.

I felt I had to leave Wall Street and did. I felt that the head injuries had knocked me off the rails. Little things, little challenges would knock me off balance.

I was frightened that I would never be able to succeed and that I wouldn't be able to cope with civilian life, though I was anxious to get back to it.

I didn't know it then, but I was experiencing symptoms of post-traumatic stress disorder, or PTSD.

I tried a series of other jobs, briefly selling freezers and then vacation homes and reporting on baseball games.

None stuck.

Some success, but more of the same

I then embarked on a three-year career in entertainment, mostly playing guitar and singing folk songs at school assembly programs. I loved it.

One reason I went into the entertainment business was to prove to myself that artistic ability, as one example of intelligence, was not necessarily inherited, that it could be learned.

In elementary school I had been classified as a "listener" for music lessons — somebody who had no musical talent and who was therefore not entitled to any musical lessons. So, being somewhat of a rebel, I decided to work at it. To prove I could develop musical talent. I practiced and practiced. Then I practiced more. Playing and singing nine hours a day in three three-hour shifts.

I was enjoying success in my musical entertainment career, scheduling more and more school performances.

As we all know, though, life often has its own rhythm and turns.

During this time, I fell in love and got married. And while my wife, who I adored, was pregnant with our second child, she was no longer willing to travel with me. So I decided to accept the generous offer by her father and brother of a job and ultimate partnership in their surplus cutting-tool business in Los Angeles.

But in this case too, after three years, things did not work out.

I was having trouble getting along with my brother-in-law in business.

So in 1960 I decided it was best to leave L.A. and open, with their support, my own tool company in South San Francisco.

There, on a sunny afternoon, after having purchased some large high-speed surplus drills from the Navy in Vallejo, I had stopped at a traffic light. Suddenly, a truck crashed into me from behind, jolting my head.

That car accident triggered for me a severe case of PTSD.

Going to and from work each day, I had to pass the San Francisco Airport. Following this accident, whenever a plane would fly overhead, I would panic and have to pull off the road.

Learning coping skills
Knowing I needed help in dealing with my PTSD, I went for outpatient treatment to the Veterans Administration hospital in Menlo Park, Calif.

There, under supervision by the head psychologist, John Marquis, I first learned relaxation techniques — I learned to relax my muscles, maintain attention on a task despite distractions, and consciously direct my motivation. I also developed memory skills and took a speed-reading class.

I soon tried out my new learning skills at a local university. I got all A's, evidencing skill levels far superior to even my pre-head-injury levels.

With that success as further motivation, I then enrolled in a master's program for a school psychology credential. And, a couple of years later, after receiving my M.S. in educational counseling, I enrolled in a Ph.D. program in learning at the University of Washington.

Exploring the components of intelligence
Prior to beginning at the university, while I was being treated at the VA clinic in Menlo Park, I tutored four young kindergarten-age children once a week in a private volunteer school for low-income, learning-challenged children. Because I was new at it, I was given two boys and two girls who were the most difficult and poor learners and who wouldn't fit into the regular classes.

My four progressed very rapidly, to the point where the school president sent two other teachers to observe our class. I reinforced most of my students' little successes with M&M's. The two teachers who were observing me thought they were doing the same, but they were using large chunks of gooey candy over an inch cubed.

Many of these children had had no breakfast, and my hunch is that the large doses of sugar made them feel ill and distracted. That was not helping them learn or feel encouraged about doing good work.

As I considered it long afterwards, the small reinforcing rewards were productive. I used only M&M's and, after a bit of progress, would reduce that to half of an M&M. Often I would give the other half to myself, rub my tummy and say, "Yum, yum, yum." This caused my little students to giggle and laugh, and I joined with them. Not only were they getting reinforced for learning, they were relaxing and having a good time in a classroom for the first time.

It was this wonderful experience, perhaps more than any other, that caused me to begin to wonder whether intelligence was not, as I had been taught, 90 percent inherited, but, in fact, very plastic, perhaps even a readily improvable skill. These four youngsters were treated in their schools as intellectually disabled. Yet when relaxed and enjoying themselves, they learned at least at a normal rate.

As part of my doctoral studies at U of W, I formally explored the idea that intelligence might be or might become a skill. What became evident to me was that it could become a skill when it was analyzed into its components, and when those components were understood well enough to convert each of them into skills.

I conducted a number of studies testing the idea with children and adults and presented four papers on the subject at two school psychology conventions.

Breaking down the terms

Two definitions of what I mean by "intelligence" and "skill" might be helpful here before going on.

What, according to my understanding, is intelligence? It is the ability to learn. But it is a very broad ability to learn. As it is commonly understood it is the ability to acquire new facts, concepts and ideas, but it also includes acquiring new feelings, attitudes and behaviors; and, perhaps above all, new habits in all of those dimensions.

And what is a skill? The best way to understand "skill" is to compare it to "process" and "ability." A process, according to the American Heritage Dictionary of the English Language is: "A series of actions, changes or functions bringing about a result" (such as digestion). An ability is an acquirable and improvable process. A skill is an ability that is improvable to a high degree and, in many cases, best assumed to be infinitely improvable since new methods and understandings often allow a skill to become more and more improvable.

Our increasing understanding over the past century of intelligence and its component elements now allows us to convert it from a complex learning ability (an acquirable and improvable process) into a complex learning skill, one that you and I and almost everyone can, with a very high probability of success, improve to significantly and substantially higher, more productive levels.

Beginning with Chapter 2, you will find a step-by-step guide to improving the component skills of intelligence, an approach I have termed Skilligence®.

But first, a little more on why this is so important.

The need

The human animal's need for a higher level of intelligence (learning ability) has grown slowly since at least 30,000 years ago, when the domesticated dog may have evolved from the wolf. We began as hunter-gatherers, moving through primitive and then modern farming, and through the industrial revolution's mass-production labor requirements.

In recent decades, however, the need for higher levels of learning ability has begun to grow at an accelerating rate.

Our society is evolving and shifting — more and more we are required to have increasingly sophisticated skills to be successful at work, at careers that are demanding intensifying technological facility. And because of that, there's a growing need for individuals with more powerful learning abilities to cope and thrive in the modern economy.

As noted in a report by the SHRM Foundation titled "What's Next:

Future Global Trends Affecting Your Organization," published by The Economist Intelligence Unit in February 2014, inequality is rising as technology renders the mid-skilled tier of workers virtually irrelevant:

"Technological advances have also automated many routine tasks formerly performed by mid-skilled workers. At the same time, companies bemoan a shortage of highly skilled workers in certain positions, such as technical workers and the senior executives entrusted with corporate decision-making. With automation of jobs set to expand further as technology advances, and a persistent skills deficit for specialized jobs, inequality is likely to increase, raising widespread concerns about social and political stability."

In other words, if we don't adjust, economic inequality will increase, as will social and political instability.

The ability to learn that was adequate for modest human survival 1,000 years ago and even 100 years ago is no longer nearly adequate to cope well in a modern economy. A significantly and substantially higher level of intelligence has now become absolutely necessary for comfortable living, and, indeed for many, for survival.

Perhaps most critical is that the destructive power of weapons has also accelerated — perhaps the fastest of all. They can now destroy substantially all life on Earth. Exactly how members of the human community will create a weapons-free world before some accident or craziness destroys us, I do not know. What I do know is that it will require the interaction of many wiser and more dedicated individuals than now exist to design and structure a world governance capable of making and keeping peace and eliminating weapons of mass destruction. I dedicate this work to my family, to my coworkers, and to those potential people.

THE BASICS OF SKILLIGENCE

The skills

The good news is it is not terribly difficult for most human beings to increase their learning ability. And when they do, it is hugely freeing.

It may take a little or a lot of time, but it can be accomplished with a very high degree of confidence. If you need to dig a big hole, it's worth the time to go to the store and get a good shovel or borrow one from your neighbor.

If you would like to progress in or learn a new career, it is, in the same way, well worth taking the time and giving the effort to strengthen your learning ability.

A highly respected therapist who worked with people with head injuries once said to me that intelligence has an infinite number of components. That, or something close to it, may well be true. But the

Skilligence system, which breaks it into 10 components, surely includes or encapsulates most of them.

And working with those component skills, for most people, will result in individual improvements that will bring lasting life-enhancing benefits.

So, in short, in the Skilligence system, intelligence is composed of 10 skills. Broken down further, there are four Basic Skills, two Core Skills and four Higher Order Skills.

The four Basic Skills are: Relaxation, Attention, Motivation and Memory.

The two Core Skills are: Communications and Computations.

The four Higher Order Skills are: Concept Formation, Problem Solving, Creativity, and Precision Learning.

Each of these 10 skills are significantly and substantially improvable. And when each improves, intelligence improves.

(Note: To be clear, each of the 10 components only becomes an improvable skill when you have developed an understanding of it.)

The foundation four

There is one other part to the whole Skilligence system, and I call that its "Foundation," the base upon which, and within which, the 10 skills operate. This Foundation includes: Inheritance, Trial-and-Error, Imitation and Instruction.

I do not consider these four to be skills. They are processes, abilities and habits that are necessary for dependable learning.

Human beings, like other animals, learn many things through inheritance: moving, hugging, the startle response, breathing, making sounds, sucking, and seeing, for several examples.

Then, through trial-and-error, we refine those processes and, for example, learn to walk erect. Through imitation we learn to run, and finally, for athletic competition, through a coach's instruction, we may learn to run faster and longer or play basketball or tennis, baseball, volleyball or football.

At higher levels of a sport or skill, we again resort to trial-and-error for small increments of improvement. Learning to become aware of and to take advantage of our inherited behaviors and tendencies, as well as building familiarity and facility with using trial-and-error, imitation and instruction to acquire new and improved levels of skills, is the hallmark of a highly intelligent human being.

When acquisition of career skills or a body of knowledge is important to us, we are wise to seek instruction from the most competent teachers available and to imitate several of the most skilled in our chosen area.

GETTING STARTED

In each of the following 10 chapters, one of the 10 skills will be introduced. You will learn how each skill contributes to intelligence, how improvable the skill appears to be and how to improve it, and then how to integrate it into your overall learning ability.

The final chapter will offer some further suggestions for acquisition, implementation and use of the integrated higher level skill with some emphasis on initiating and developing the chunking habit — the process of breaking down a difficult task into small pieces, where each piece is easy to learn and accomplish —avoiding the often overwhelming expectation of being able to learn everything at once.

Final note: It is very helpful, as you develop each skill, to have chosen a learning challenge to try it out on. That will help entrench and integrate each increment of the higher skill you develop.

CHAPTER TWO

SKILL 1: RELAXATION

Relaxation techniques are a valuable tool often used as a method to reduce stress. They are recommended by such well-regarded institutions as the Mayo Clinic, Harvard Medical School and the National Institutes for Health. Relaxation is often utilized as a therapy for post-traumatic stress disorder. Some studies have even found it to have a beneficial effect on heart disease, headaches and pain management, and ongoing studies are looking into its effect in other areas of mental and physical health.

Within Skilligence, the Relaxation skill is the foundation stone of intelligence building — it is the base upon which the other nine component skills of intelligence rest and depend.

Our aim in developing the Relaxation skill is threefold:

1) To gain the ability to get deeply relaxed whenever you want or need to, and relatively independently of your environment at the time;

2) To be able to develop a high level of energy when you want to without interfering tensions;

3) To be able to develop a pleasant level of energy and muscle tension that is approximately optimum for your learning task.

The Relaxation skill contributes to intelligence in three different ways: first, by supporting the healing of physical ills; second, by helping to reduce and remove anxiety and phobic responses that interfere with learning; third, by matching your muscle tension level and other elements of arousal to the complexity and familiarity, or unfamiliarity, of your learning task.

It can be used and practiced somewhat differently for each purpose.

In support of healing
Edmund Jacobson's book "You Must Relax," written early in the last century, explains how Relaxation helps to heal and prevent many physical ills. A physician, he invented his technique, called "progressive relaxation therapy," to help his patients deal with anxiety.

It is important when using deep muscle relaxation for healing purposes to remain deeply relaxed for at least 20 minutes, for it takes that long for the involuntary muscles to imitate the relaxed voluntary muscles.

It is helpful to practice relaxation about three times a week over a period of several months for real healing and prevention to take place.

Regulating arousal
Through muscle relaxation, we can regulate arousal, the most basic and most pervasive of all life processes.

Arousal is the physiological state of being awake, alert and attentive.

At an ideal arousal state for most tasks, including learning tasks, you feel energetic with no interfering tensions. Recall when you were the most engaged in a challenging, fun task. Embed that feeling in your memory. Retrieve and re-create it from now on whenever you tackle a learning challenge.

To the degree that our arousal is out of synch with the needs of the learning task at hand, our learning ability diminishes. When our arousal is appropriate, our learning ability is at its optimum level.

By developing our muscle relaxation skill, we can approximate an optimum arousal for each challenge, and as we do, our learning ability — and our potential for improving our intelligence — soars.

Dispelling anxiety

There are a number of ways to rid yourself of anxiety and phobic responses. One popular procedure is called "Eye Movement Desensitization and Reprocessing"; another is meditation.

A discussion of either is beyond the scope of this workbook, but both techniques usually work well in displacing anxiety and phobic responses, especially when administered by a trained therapist.

For more serious problems like PTSD and entrenched phobic responses, deep muscle relaxation and desensitization is a more thorough approach, although using all three approaches with a skilled therapist may well be ideal. You may also consider use of diaphragm breathing and meditation — these last two are additional techniques to help lower anxieties.

One illustration of how relaxation and systematic desensitization can work in difficult cases involves a postman who had been attacked on his route by a large dog. He would panic at the thought of going back to that house and even onto the street. But when he was assigned to a desk job, he didn't like it, so he asked for help to get back on his route.

I gave him instructions in deep muscle relaxation over a period of time. Then I asked him to tell me how close he could imagine himself getting to the house where the attack took place and still feel perfectly comfortable. It turned out to be several long blocks away.

One day, after he had learned to relax following several weeks of Deep Muscle Relaxation Training, I asked him to become deeply relaxed and to signal me when he was. Then I asked him to visualize the place several blocks away where he said he was completely comfortable. I did this twice and when he reported that he could picture that clearly with no disturbance, I asked him to picture himself carrying his mail bag from there, one block closer.

He was unable to do that without feeling anxiety again. So we tried imagining going just a half-block closer, and that was successful. I asked him to do this several times until he could picture it at least twice in succession with no disturbance at all.

Over a period of a couple of months, he moved gradually closer to the house with the dog in his visualizations, mostly in half-block increments. On the last block, however, we had to move closer just a few feet at a time and over a period of several weeks. But finally he was able to imagine himself delivering mail comfortably to the house with the dog again. Before he actually returned to work, I went with him and we traversed the same route a couple of times slowly in reality. After just a couple of times, he was comfortable taking the route himself, able to relax and not rush through it.

Small steps
The secret of success with this technique is deep, deep muscle relaxation and then progressing in as many tiny steps as are necessary to succeed with desensitization. With milder anxieties, the steps can be larger.

This is a good technique to use when you are disturbed and trying to learn something — for example, if you have an anxiety response when you think of studying algebra or taking an algebra test.

Exercise

Practicing relaxation

To experience deep muscle relaxation, practice tensing and then relaxing almost every one of your voluntary muscles, one at a time, from the largest one in your buttocks to the tiny ones around your eyes and tongue.

First, learn to tighten and relax the muscles in your arms, then the other large muscles in the body, and, finally, the smaller muscles of the mouth, eyes and fingers.

Tense and hold each muscle for about six seconds and then relax for about 10 to 20 seconds. Feel the relaxation in that muscle and feel the relaxation spread to other muscles in the body.

For example, with your forearms, first tense your fists, hold and attend to the tension in your forearm for some six seconds and then relax them. Feel the relaxation in the forearms and then feel it spread. Then the same with your biceps, and then, your triceps

This is just the first part of the Relaxation process. The full process would include how to let all of your muscles get and be deeply, deeply relaxed for 20 minutes or more, and then also how to voluntarily adjust your tension to optimally match whatever challenge you may be facing.

HOW RELAXATION AIDS LEARNING

Using conscious relaxation techniques to help balance our emotional state can help boost our ability to learn.

Excessive muscle tension and arousal — as when we are in a state of fright or rage, anxiety or phobia — interrupts our brain's ability to understand and learn.

At the other end of the spectrum, laxity, torpor and depression saps our energy to learn and clouds our thinking.

Our goal, then, is moderate levels of energy and low, flexible muscle tension to most strongly support learning activities. It's a relaxed state with flexible, fluid muscles and energy.

Relaxation works through the arousal system. The arousal system is the most basic physiological process we possess. All the other physiological, emotional and mental processes depend upon it.

The nervous system normally works automatically to match an appropriate level of arousal, or alertness, to power a response to whatever behavior or learning challenge faces the individual. But sometimes this response pattern has been corrupted by one's upbringing, or even by chance, and it instead interferes with learning.

Developing the relaxation skill will help you modify arousal responses and help you create for yourself a more optimum learning environment.

Areas of research

There are at least three areas of research that further explain Relaxation's relationship to learning and, through it, to intelligence.

They are: the Rigidity of Aging, the Hierarchy of Dominant Responses and Inverted "U" Curves.

It is helpful to keep a clear understanding of these three relationships between relaxation and intelligence — this will help you become more skilled at relaxation and better able to use relaxation to increase your learning ability.

Behavior is often defined as a response to a stimulus. As we mature, our behavior — our arousal system and our responses to stimuli — evolve automatically by trial-and-error into a habit pattern for each stimulus and for each challenge.

Those stimuli may be basic, like seeing someone smile at you, or more complex, such as witnessing a fight between friends or family members.

The evolving arousal system's response is involved automatically in every behavior, in every thought, in every perception, in every emotion.

These automatic responses to such stimuli adapt over time. Some of these adaptations will be far from optimal for many current challenges, including solving new, complex family and career problems.

The rigidity of aging

The arousal system includes muscle tension. That's good news, because we can learn to voluntarily tense and relax our muscles, and the rest of the arousal system will usually follow. This permits us to alter automatically evolved arousal habits. It enables us, through control of the level of our muscle tension, to voluntarily control our arousal level. This, in turn, allows us to generate new, more adaptive behavioral responses to important challenges, ones that are more conducive to our success, like developing the learning behaviors that constitute what we call high intelligence.

Beginning in childhood, our behaviors become increasingly automatic as we begin to mature. This facilitates the development of common response habits.

It is a normal part of growing up. Our responses don't need to be reconstituted anew each time. But some of those habituated responses will not be adaptive or in our best interests to facilitate a particular new behavior. Behaviors tend to become rigid as we mature into adulthood and they continue to do so as we grow older.

Remember, this is a natural and healthy process — it assures easy and automatic responses to life's normal, everyday requirements. But when conditions change and a new response is called for, the Relaxation Skill can help you modify the arousal response and allow for greater adaptability.

Exercise
Think of some ways that your habits and behaviors may have become rigid over time and write them down in a notebook.

The Hierarchy of Dominant Responses
Related to rigidification is the theory of the Hierarchy of Dominant Responses, sometimes referred to as Habit Family Hierarchies, presented by Clark Hull and Kenneth Spence, a research team during the mid-1940s.

This theory has three parts:

First, it tells us that our responses — all of our reactions to a given stimulus — are stored in our memory system.

Second, it says that our reactions to a given stimulus are arranged in a hierarchy from "most likely to be responded" to "least likely to be responded." The responses used most often to each stimulus, and those most reinforced, become dominant and are normally and automatically responded.

And third, the higher our muscle tension level is at any one time, the less available are the responses that are low on the hierarchy. On the other hand, the lower our muscle tension and arousal level is, the broader is our available repertoire of responses.

Under maximum tension, such as rage or panic, only the most dominant response, usually flight, fight or freeze, will be available. At the other end, in contrast, under lowest muscle tension and arousal, all possible responses on the hierarchy will be available, at least via visualization.

From all of the possible behaviors we can imagine, we can choose a selected image, imitate it and, with practice, convert it into an overt, reliable behavior.

Thus, rather than having to rely on habit, with a highly developed relaxation skill our thinking brain can choose from all available responses to any challenge. Without that skill, we are virtually locked into our habit behaviors.

It makes good sense, then, that whenever you wish to make a new habit, first practice and improve your relaxation skill.

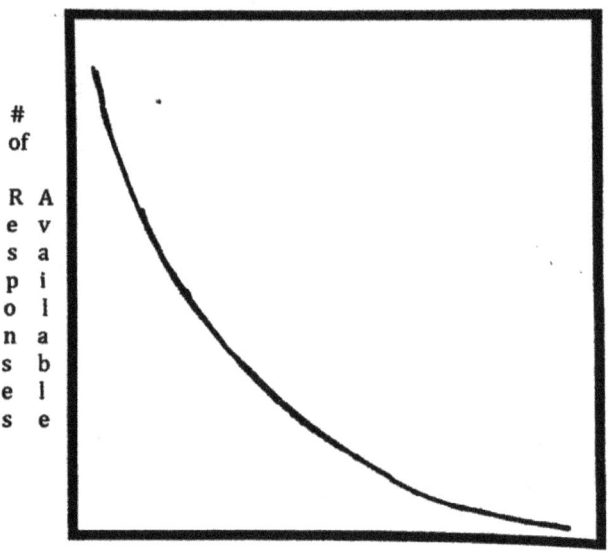

USING RELAXATION AND PRACTICE TO ACQUIRE NEW HABITS

The Relaxation skill allows us to practice new, more adaptive responses to important challenges. And through practice, we can then, in turn, create new dominant responses.

Rather than being stuck in "normal" imitation of the bad habits of our elders, this option enables us to improve how we relate at home to our children and spouses as well as in work or school environments.

First we imagine an optimum response while relaxed. Then we practice it in imagination and eventually in real life.

Exercise

Think about how you might use this understanding of Relaxation to improve your learning or another goal you'd like to accomplish. What response might you like to change using the skill of Relaxation? Write your thoughts in your notebook.

Inverted-U Curve

The Inverted-U Curve describes the relationship between arousal and muscle tension on the one hand and learning and intelligence on the other.

There are two parts to it:

a) The inverted-U curve traces the relationship from deepest, soporific levels of arousal, where no learning can take place, to modest levels of tension where learning is optimum, on to extreme high levels of tension and arousal where, again, no learning at all is possible.

In order to maximize our learning, we must first learn to initiate and maintain modest but flexible levels of tension with an energized and alert level of arousal.

b) Another important dimension to this inverted-U relationship: it changes shape according to the simplicity or complexity of the learning challenge. From simple to complex, it gets narrower.

For very simple, familiar challenges its shape is very broad. Almost any level of tension and arousal will support the simplest learning and behavior challenges.

In sharp contrast, for complex or new and strange challenges, the inverted-U curve narrows so that only a very limited and low level of muscle tension will support successful learning. For example, for learning calculus, even modest tension spikes will interfere with learning. High anxiety during this task may cause the eyes and throat muscles to spasm and almost eliminate the possibility of learning.

The Inverted "U" Curves

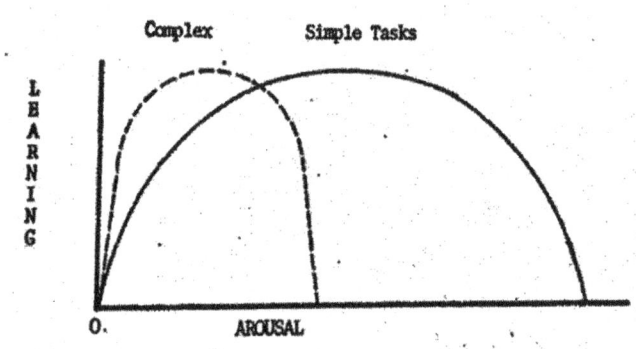

Critical relationships
These three relationships between arousal and learning — Rigidification in Aging, the Hierarchy of Dominant Responses and the Inverted "U" Curves — are the most important set to understand when it comes to achieving high-level learning and accomplishment skills.

Development of the next nine skills in the Skilligence Framework depend completely on these relationships. A thorough understanding of these three relationships between relaxation and learning will support your use of relaxation training.

These three relationships tell us that acquiring the ability to relax our muscles prior to, during and after learning is the key to increasing our intelligence. This is true particularly regarding the tiny muscles in and around the mouth — the lips, the tongue and the throat — as well as in the eyes and the fingers.

Learning to find and relax those little muscles, especially when facing an exciting and important learning challenge, is for many of us no easy task. But you can give yourself a head start by practicing deep muscle relaxation.

To practice relaxation at home, you may have someone read relaxation techniques to you or you may listen to the deep muscle relaxation CD by John Marquis (available at www.skilligence.com). Three times a week would probably be a good practice schedule for most people. You might try alternating listening to the recording one day and following it in your memory the next.

CONCLUSION AND REVIEW
1. Arousal, which includes muscle tension and relaxation, is the most basic physiological process.

2. Muscle Relaxation Skill enables us to voluntarily regulate arousal.

3. Skill in Muscle Relaxation contributes to intelligence through better physical health, through reduction of interfering anxieties and phobia, and through matching arousal level to the simplicity or complexity of the learning task.

4. Aging tends to rigidify behaviors. Relaxation skill can restore flexibility for acquiring new responses.

5. The Hierarchy of Dominant Responses tells us that our arousal level responses are stored in the memory and that under high-tension levels, only the most dominant responses are available. Achieving a high level of skill in Relaxation enables us to access the more desirable but less dominant responses.

6. The inverted-U curve demonstrates that simple learning tasks may be accomplished at almost any level of arousal and muscle tension. But complex, unfamiliar or strange learning challenges must be met with a low, flexible level of arousal. The skill of adjusting the level of tension in your muscles may be acquired through learning and practice.

7. Take plenty of time to develop a reliable Relaxation skill. A well-developed Relaxation skill combined with visualization can dissolve any automatic resistance to a desired behavior, and free you to proceed toward your goal.

Some final notes

1. We need to emphasize here that for this skill and for each of the other nine skills, we are not offering a full learning program. We are introducing the skill, explaining it and its relationship to intelligence, initiating a learning program, and enabling you to continue its development to whatever level is right for you.

2. If absorbing everything offered in this and the following nine skill chapters turns out to be a bit overwhelming, focus on just two or three parts from each that seem particularly pertinent to you. It may be optimal to work on just one skill alone for three months. Then, let the improvement seep in and solidify as you work on another for three months. Briefly review each of them on a regular basis. This will tend to subconsciously activate your use of them in your daily work and life along with the subsequent purposeful development of that skill and the expansion of your overall learning ability.

3. A reasonable recommendation is, initially, to practice relaxation three days a week for 30 to 60 minutes and in each of the other four days for five or 10 minutes.

4. You are a complex and unique individual. If you don't already have a strong background in these disciplines, develop the patience and determination to acquire and synthesize the many concepts just a little bit at a time.

5. If you'd like to get started on becoming a good relaxer on the cheap, just tense both your fists, hold them for six to 10 seconds and let them and the forearm muscles relax. Observe the feelings of relaxation and let all the other muscles in your body imitate those feelings. Enjoy the feeling of progressively deeper and deeper relaxation spreading throughout your body.

6. In our daily life, we experience many situations and challenges that trigger excessive levels of tension and arousal. One of our major life tasks is to become aware of them and then to acquire a reliable ability to return ourselves to an approximately optimum level of tension and arousal for whatever our current challenge might be.

REFERENCES & RESOURCES

Benson, Herbert, M.D. and Proctor, William, J.D., Relaxation Revolution.; New York, NY: Scribner, 2010.

Davis, Martha, Ph.D.; Eshelman, Elizabeth Robinson, M.S.W.; McKay, Mathew, Ph.D., The Relaxation & Stress Reduction Workbook 5th Edition. Oakland, Calif.: New Harbinger, 1980.

Jacobson, Edmund, M.D. , You Must Relax. , M.D.; New York, NY: McGraw-Hill, 1964.

Marquis, John N. Ph.D., Deep Muscle Relaxation CD (available at skilligenceworkshops.com).

Marquis, John N.; Morgan, Wesley G.; Piaget, Gerald W., A Guidebook for Systematic Desensitization. Palo Alto, Calif. : Veterans Workshop, Veterans Administration Hospital, 1971.

Rose, Menko, Modification of Manifested Intelligence Through Relaxation Training in the Classroom. Master's Thesis, CSU-Hayward, Calif., 1969.

CHAPTER THREE

SKILL 2: ATTENTION

In studying Attention, I have found that this skill is, in fact, much more complex than it initially appears.
The American Heritage Dictionary of the English language defines Attention as: "Concentration of the mental powers upon an object; a close or careful observing or listening," to which I would add at the end, "or smell or touch or taste."

Among its many dimensions are:
  Attention span
  Focus
  Orienting response
  Habituation
  Vigilance
  Startle response
  Resilience
  Clarity
  Sharpness
  Resistance to distraction
  Re-attending
  Keeping your goal in mind

Those who study learning and the mind consider the ability to attend to be an essential element. Researchers have been in agreement about that fact for a long time.

As far back as 1907, E.B. Titchener named attention as the central nerve of the entire psychological system. While in 1963, researchers Zeaman and House identified attention as the factor that discriminates between the intellectually disabled and normal students. In 1967, J.K. Hewitt ranked attention on a hierarchy of learning abilities as the most fundamental.

What all of this means is, if you'd like to strengthen your intelligence, it will be key to:

Pay attention to Attention.

And, take time to improve the skill.

How is Attention related to intelligence?
The Attention skill is as crucial to learning ability as Relaxation is. Like Relaxation, it is also inextricably intertwined with every other process, behavior and ability that make up intelligence.

You will find that each component, each skill acts back on the others to help improve intelligence.

Developing your Attention skill requires practicing attention exercises. It also requires developing an understanding of attention, including knowledge of its many dimensions. That knowledge will aid in its improvement.

For example, it's important to understand is that while Attention is a prerequisite to Motivation, Motivation is a prerequisite to optimum development of the Attention skill. That motivation must be focused for at least several minutes several times a week to practice attention exercises.

The other skills further up the Skilligence hierarchy are also involved in improving the Attention skill.

For example, figuring out the best way to develop your Attention skill is a Problem Solving process. Thinking of yourself as a good, motivated student and a worthy person — that is, having self-worth as a smart and capable student — is a Concept Formation process and is also integral to developing a good Attention skill. And, finally, it is your Memory that reminds you precisely how a good Attention skill will benefit you and how to go about improving it.

But then, you would have to remember to focus your attention on that Memory in order to use it.

Is it possible to improve Attention?
Obviously, there are many ways to improve Attention, at least as many as there are dimensions. But still, Attention seems hard to put your finger on. In his 1969 book, Moray, a prominent British researcher on attention, stated that although research on practiced attention has not been done, it is almost certain that performance of practiced subjects "will differ by orders of magnitude" from that of unpracticed subjects. He wrote, "What is not usually published is that it is common for experimenters in the field of attention to find after some time that they can achieve performance levels in competitive and selective [attention] tasks which far exceed the performance levels attained by their subjects."

So, Attention is a critical component of intelligence and it is hugely improvable.

HOW DO YOU IMPROVE ATTENTION?
Following are exercises that, over time, will help you to far exceed your current Attention skill. This, in turn, may well increase your overall learning ability by orders of magnitude.

The best way to build Attention is to do it in small steps. First you attend well for a short period on a simple, interesting target. (For example, a set of numbers.) Then register that experience, that feeling, in your memory. Then, very gradually, attend clearly and well for slightly longer periods, and then onto slightly more complex and difficult targets, say a longer string of numbers. Always be careful to achieve several successes at one level before taking on the next, slightly more difficult level.

At first, in order to experience a high level of attention, remember clearly an experience of attending to something that completely captured your attention, perhaps a book you particularly enjoyed reading. Then transfer that attention response onto a new learning challenge.

Practice this transfer frequently and regularly until your attention response to learning challenges becomes reliable and sustainable. This simple exercise usually works very well.

Exercise 1
Think of one thing now — something that completely captured your attention. Record your response in a notebook.

Exercise 2
When you're out walking, glance at a car's license plate and then look away. Practice attending briskly and see if you can replicate the license number — without closing your eyes.
If you have trouble recalling the entire number, practice with just the last three digits. Then try the whole plate.
When you have success at one plate, try for one plate plus the last three digits of another. After a number of successes at that level, try two full plates. This will help you develop a reliable ability to focus sharp attention quickly on a new target.

The following instruction from *The Attention Revolution* by B. Alan Wallace is another worthwhile and workable attention exercise.

He writes:

"Please get comfortable, back straight, arms and hands resting on your knees, head upright or slightly forward. Relax and be at ease. Be still. Be vigilant. These three qualities of the body are to be maintained throughout all meditation sessions. Once you have settled your body with these three qualities, take three slow, gentle, deep breaths, breathing in and out through the nostrils. Let your awareness permeate your entire body as you do so, noting any sensations that arise in relation to the respiration. Luxuriate in these breaths, as if you were receiving a gentle massage from within.

"Breathing through your nostrils, focus your attention on how your breath feels as it first fills your diaphragm, then your stomach and then your chest and then exhale, letting all the muscles of your body relax more and more. Return your attention to your breath going in and out of your body whenever distractions intervene, completely accepting the intervention as a natural event."

Wallace suggests doing this meditation exercise for 24 minutes as the initial stage (of 10 stages) of your Attention skill development. I started with 10 minutes.

Using attention to improve Attention

Once you have at least a modestly high-level Attention response, try doing an easy Sudoku puzzle. Sudokus are normally thought of as a problem-solving challenge, but once you learn how to do them, they are primarily an exerciser for your Attention skill.

In fact, Sudoku puzzles are an excellent Attention exercise. The harder ones do require some bit of an advanced Attention skill to solve.

You can also find good exercises of various kinds designed to improve Attention and Memory on the Internet.

An important book on the subject of attention is *The Flame of Attention*, by Jiddu Krishnamurti, about overcoming psychological anxiety.

According to Krishnamurti, attention can be used to improve Attention.

Attend to a disturbance — for example, the feelings of anxiety, depression, distractibility that interfere with learning — and your attention will dissolve that disturbance and leave your learning ability free to thrive. For a long-entrenched disturbance, I've found this technique works best in combination with deep-muscle relaxation in order to weaken the disturbing response.

For example, for many people, math test anxiety is a common and often disabling problem. Although it could be non-existent three weeks prior, the day just before the exam it might be so intense that one's thinking and calculating abilities are obliterated.

In order to weaken the anxiety response, the trick is to first make a hierarchy of small steps to practice. It could be a series of math tests, from easy to difficult. Or it could be imagining yourself progressing from a time distant from the test to a time close to the test. Steps should be small. For example, if you're imagining yourself progressing, start three weeks before, then, for example, you might step to 2.5 weeks, 2 weeks, 1.5 weeks, 1.25 weeks, 1 week, 5 days, 3 days, 2 days, the day before, the morning before.

Lie back in a comfortable chair. Get deeply, deeply relaxed under secure, non-threatening, non-disturbing conditions at least three, and preferably more weeks beforehand. Then, imagine yourself three weeks before the test for about 10 seconds. A successful trial is when you feel absolutely no anxiety. After three successful tries, do the same but this time imagining yourself two-and-a-half weeks before. Proceed in this manner through the hierarchy, always succeeding three times before moving to the next step.

Above all, attend to this problem thoroughly and well beforehand for a likely successful outcome. If it turns out to be very difficult to achieve a programmed step, just move back a step or divide that step into several smaller steps.

SUMMARY

In sum, three great avenues for improving the Attention skill are:

(1) Imagine and then practice clear, sharp attention for short periods on easy targets and then gradually for longer periods on more challenging targets.

(2) Remove (or dispel) negative influences like depression, rage, distractibility, anxieties and other disturbances;

(3) Practice exercises like remembering license plates or doing Sudokus or find a few others on the Internet.

In addition, reading several of the good books on Attention, focusing and mindfulness may suggest additional ways, some more suited to your nature, for developing a high-quality, dependable Attention skill.

Successful accomplishers firmly reject distractions — and keep their goal in mind at all times.

Takeaways
Much of your Attention skill development likely will be determined by your specific motivation to do so. And that will depend partly on the need you feel for a more powerful learning ability and, in turn, your understanding of attention's key place in the intelligence hierarchy.

So, give some consideration to identifying the considerable benefits an improved learning ability may bring you: A better job with higher pay, for example. Set and keep the goal of an improved intelligence prominently in your mind. Then let this goal pull you powerfully into the attention-building activities you choose.

The most important takeaway from this chapter is this: if your Attention skill is low, you are able to improve it.

Motivating yourself to move on
A change in self-concept — for example, "I am a growing, changing person, improving my most important life skills" — may be another critical factor in Attention development. You may find that saying this to yourself, rehearsing it while looking at yourself in the mirror daily, will cause your Attention skill to grow remarkably and dependably.

As you move on to the next chapter, "Motivation," and other subsequent chapters and skills, be sure to continue your practice of Relaxation, and review material from the first chapter and this one on Attention.

You might also want to think ahead about the reasons you would like to improve your learning ability, and how important it is for you to be able to regularly motivate yourself to improve your learning ability.

As an adult, you can schedule your own reinforcers as your attention improves. Reinforce, or reward, yourself for small Attention skill improvements.

More attention builders
And finally, here are five suggestions to add to your growing repertoire of attention-building activities and inspirations:

1. Remind yourself regularly that being distracted is normal. Practice re-attending with a sharp, clear focus, so that you have that reliable habit readily available whenever you need it.

2. "True education is directed at formation of the focused mind and the ability to think clearly. ... A focused mind, in turn, may result in financial success and personal happiness, depending on how one uses that developed faculty." —John E. Wall

3. "The greatest gift you can give another is the purity of your attention." — Richard Moss

4. "There are two forms of attention. One is open and global; you light on many different aspects of your surroundings for short periods of time. Open attention gives you an overall impression of your environment. ...

"The second form of attention is more focused — you concentrate on one thing for long periods. Focused attention requires active filtering of excess information, and you notice details in sequences rather than all at once.

Whereas global attention is like an overhead light, focused attention is like a flashlight with a narrow beam. ... Everyone needs both of these types of attention." —Barbara Sher, in the introduction to *Attention Games*

5. Reinforcers, or rewards, are our final suggestion for improving your attention. (See also Ch. 11, Precision Learning.)

For example, consider the Attention Training System created by Michael Gordon, Ph.D., for teachers: "This sensible approach to enhancing attention involves a small battery-operated electronic counter which is placed on the student's desk. The ATS automatically awards the child a point every 60 seconds. If the student wanders off task, the teacher uses remote control to deduct a point and activate a small warning light on the student's module. The ATS delivers unobtrusive but effective feedback, functions during regular classroom activities, circumvents the problem of treatment generalization, and has been shown to be as effective as stimulant medication in increasing attentiveness. Each teacher can control four student modules."

≈≈≈≈≈

"In an era of unstoppable distractions ... now more than ever we must learn to sharpen focus if we are to contend with, let along thrive in, a complex world."
—From the cover of *Focus* by Daniel Goleman

≈≈≈≈≈

REFERENCES & RESOURCES

Attention Training Institute, www.attentiontraininginstitute.com.

Cardillo, Joseph, *Can I Have Your Attention? How to Think Fast, Find Your Focus, and Sharpen your Concentration*, Pompton Plains, NJ: Career Press, 2009.

Flora, Sherrill B., *Pay Attention, Please! Games and Activities to Improve Attention, Focus & Listening Skills*, 2010.

Goleman, Daniel, *Focus: the Hidden Drivers of Excellence*, New York, NY: Harper, 2013. (Explores myriad ways in which high-level attention and focus skills are requisite components of intelligence and a good life.)

Gordon, Michael, Ph.D., Attention Training System Starter Package, www.addwarehouse.com

Krishnamurti, *The Flame of Attention*. New York, NY: Harper, 1984.

Lumosity, enhance memory and attention, www.lumosity.com.

MCT Institute, www.mct-institute.com/attention-training-technique.html.

Sher, Barbara, *Attention Games*. Hoboken, NJ: Jossey-Bass, 2006.

Wallace, B. Alan, *The Attention Revolution: Unlocking the Power of the Focused Mind*. Boston, MA: Wisdom Publications, 2006.

CHAPTER FOUR

SKILL 3: MOTIVATION

In this chapter, you'll be reading much about Motivation, the third skill on the Skilligence hierarchy after Relaxation and Attention.

While working on Motivation, the two critical habits that will benefit you most are:

1. Keeping your goal in mind at all times

and

2. Regularly practicing seeing yourself successfully accomplishing small, easy steps toward your goal.

Repeat these two critical habits to yourself and observe how the process makes you feel.

What is Motivation?

The American Heritage Dictionary of the English Language gives three definitions for "motivate," the verb tense of motivation: 1) to provide with an incentive; 2) to move to action; 3) to impel.

I think of Motivation as an inner force that moves us to act toward a goal.

How is Motivation related to intelligence?

In the early 1960s, the controversial Arthur Jensen at U.C. Berkeley claimed that his research demonstrated that determination and persistence were the keys to high creativity, far more important than an IQ level over 120.

Motivation — which incorporates determination and persistence — is also the key to intelligence. If you cultivate your curiosity, your determination and your persistence, and consistently funnel them into the Motivation to learn, your learning skills will continue to increase. And that's without specific, systematic skill development. Adding specific, systematic skill development will complement and accelerate that progress.

Make your Motivation to learn the highest priority
Pause for a moment and imagine the Motivation to learn. Did you feel it? Repeat this visualization until you can actually feel the words, not just think them.

Although Motivation (as indicated on the Skilligence® hierarchy) is prerequisite to the higher seven skills, all nine of the other skills contribute to an effective Motivation. For example, if our concept of ourselves is that we are stupid and foggy-brained, our Motivation will be weak and ineffective, and we will be blown about by the lightest of breezes (distractions). If, on the other hand, we regularly practice seeing ourselves as bright, involved and highly motivated, our Motivation is likely to be strong and effective. As another example, our problem-solving skills will help us design and schedule our development of a reliable Motivation.

As you can imagine, Motivation is crucial to the process of increasing your learning ability — maintaining the determination to keep practicing exercises and improving your skills.

Exercise

As you read through this chapter, and even the entire book, think regularly of the following question and make notes of your answers: What can I do during the study of this book to help motivate myself to regularly work at increasing my overall learning ability?
Write your answers in your notebook.

FACTORS AFFECTING MOTIVATION
Each of these factors may be important to you at different times, so try to finish this chapter with a solid understanding of each.

1. Fear of Failure
2. Perseverance vs. Perseveration
3. Ambivalence
4. Hierarchy of Needs
5. Self-Reinforcement
6. Chunking
7. Behavior Affects Emotion
8. Self-Perception
9. Perception of the Outside World
10. Attitude
11. Task perception
12. Prioritizing
13. Self-talk

This is a big list. But Motivation is crucial to life and to intelligence building. Gather an introductory idea of each dimension on this list, but then choose just one or two that may be important to you at this time in your life and thoroughly absorb and work on them initially.

There are other factors as well that affect Motivation, including expectations, anxieties and phobias, and things that may have happened in your past (check out the book "*When the Past Is Present*, by David Richo).

You can probably think of other factors that might affect your Motivation.

This chapter will expand on many of these dimensions but be sure to do your own research on others.

1) Fear of Failure
While fear of failure may be stimulating when mild, it is very destructive when excessive. In fact, I am convinced that an excessive fear of failure is the most common, ever-present and pervasive, yet preventable block to learning ability. The best approach is to try to identify it, become aware of it whenever it rears its ugly head. Don't run away from it.

Use deep muscle relaxation and/or *The Flame of Attention* to help diminish and remove it, while also using your Concept Formation skill to substitute and strengthen the "I am succeeding in small steps" self-image to replace the fear of failure.

If as a child, or an adult for that matter, you were beaten or shamed when you did something wrong, you may well be plagued by a strong fear of failure. This fear may have a strong negative impact on your ability to learn, say, math, because mathematics depends to a great extent on trial-and-error learning. Such early hurts will also have great impact on social and relationship learning, which also relies much on trial-and-error learning. Furthermore, when you leave the classroom for the wide, wide world of work, you will find much to learn by trial-and-error.

Often, to compensate for our fear of failure, we create a false self-image. That image is easily fragmented because little missteps can raise the scepter of big missteps and the possibility of failure. And then, even when recovered, we are left vulnerable. So, it is critically important, in order to assure successful learning and accomplishment that we overcome this fear of failure and embrace the concept of learning by trial-and-error.

In order to help overcome fear of failure, one can learn to think of failure as a normal part of the learning and accomplishing process, to take each of many failures as an opportunity to learn how not to do it, acknowledging that you are that much closer to success. Relaxation and desensitization, as well as eye movement desensitization and reprocessing, are also two proven methods of relieving anxiety about failure. Skilled practitioners are most likely available in your area. It is important to be aware that habituating and removing negative habits of perception and action is just as important, in many instances, as building positive elements of Motivation.

In the meanwhile, remind yourself frequently and regularly of what Thomas Edison said: "I have not failed. I've just found ten thousand ways that won't work."

And that's the perseverance to which we may all aspire.

2) Perseverance versus perseveration

While perseverance (persistence at a task or toward a goal despite difficulty or delay in achieving success) is a key element of high-grade Motivation, in rigid extreme it becomes "perseveration." Perseveration (inappropriate and uncontrollable repetition of a particular response even in the absence of the original stimulus) takes all the muscles engaged in persevering and ties them into big knots, imprisoning any possibility of accomplishing any real learning.

Nevertheless, the gradual building of the sustained, modest power to persevere toward a worthy goal, despite obstacles and failures, is a critical component of the Motivation facet of intelligence.

It pays to have a list of strong reinforcements to support strengthening your power and confidence to persevere. For one, even brief Attention to the progress resulting when you do persevere is a powerful and reliable reinforcement.

3) Ambivalence

In his book *The Will to Live*, Arnold Hutschnecker explains the pervasiveness of ambivalence — that for every positive motivation, we have a corresponding negative one, including the will to live and the will to die.

For the purposes of this book, we may have a will to learn but also a will to not learn, or a will to succeed and a will to fail.

Become aware of your own ambivalences. When you observe your feelings and perceptions, do you find that you have ambivalent feelings about your will to learn and to increase your intelligence?

Remember to melt the negatives away with deep muscle relaxation and Krishnamurti's Flame of Attention — that is, focusing your attention on that negative thought, on that disturbance, to dispel it. At the same time, rehearse, reinforce and strengthen an entrenched, sustained urge — in essence, to create a strong enduring habit — to acquire a powerful learning ability. It helps to keep your goal in mind.

Exercise

Take a moment to put your thoughts in writing
on the following:
What reasons or feelings do you have to learn well?
What reasons do you have to learn poorly or to not learn?
What steps can you take to strengthen your will to learn?

4) Maslow's (and our) Hierarchy of Needs

Psychologist Abraham Maslow first introduced his concept of a Hierarchy of Needs in his 1943 paper "A Theory of Human Motivation" and in his subsequent book, *Motivation and Personality*. His hierarchy suggests that people are strongly and probably innately motivated to fulfill basic needs before moving on to other, more advanced needs.

His hierarchy is most often displayed as a pyramid. The lowest levels of the pyramid are made up of the most basic needs, while the more complex needs are located at the top of the pyramid. Needs at the bottom of the pyramid are basic, physical, survival requirements including the need for food, water, sleep and warmth.

Once these lower-level needs have been met, people tend to move on to the next level of needs, which are for safety and security, including financial and emotional security.

As people progress up the pyramid, needs become increasingly psychological and social. Soon, the need for love, for friendship and for intimacy become important. Still further up the pyramid, the need for personal esteem and feelings of accomplishment take priority. Like Carl Rogers, Maslow emphasized self-actualization, which is a process of growing and developing as a person in order to achieve and expand one's "individual potential" — the feeling of expanding and growing.

Understanding Maslow's Hierarchy of Needs will add significantly to one's self-understanding and self-acceptance.

These needs exert a strong and sometimes subliminal pull on us, often constructive but sometimes inhibiting. You may want to consider your own needs: Where are you now on that hierarchy? How do they affect what you are currently attempting? How important to you is your intelligence? How will you accept, coordinate and harness all these needs in a constructive fashion?

Maslow's Hierarchy of Needs

HIGHER NEEDS
Self-actualization
Feelings of Accomplishment
Personal Esteem

INTERMEDIATE NEEDS
Love
Friendship
Intimacy

BASIC NEEDS
Food
Water
Sleep
Warmth
Add Financial Independence and Freedom from Pain

Exercise
(Write your answers in your notebook.)
What are your primary needs at this point in your life?
How might your needs boost or impede your motivation to build your intelligence?

5) Skinner and reinforcement
The most powerful and dependable single tool for increasing and strengthening our motivation, accomplishment and learning, I believe, is Self-Reinforcement. (Self-Reinforcing is covered additionally in the Precision Learning chapter.)

B.F. Skinner's most famous work was with pigeons. When a pigeon would turn its head slightly to the right, Skinner would reward it with a kernel of grain. He would do this a couple of times. Then he would only reward the bird if it turned farther in that same direction. The pigeon would randomly experiment until it did turn farther and then still farther until, finally, Skinner would only reward it when it turned a complete circle. In this way in small steps, he taught the pigeon to behave in a manner completely foreign to its nature, which testified to the power of systematic reinforcement. And it works quite as well when we apply it to ourselves when we wish to substitute one habit for another.

Skinner refined his procedures, finding that once the behavior was learned, gradually more intermittent reinforcing (at first, every success, then every other one, then every third, etc.) was more powerful in cementing the behavior. This understanding has been used to help handicapped children learn and Ph.D. students to finish their dissertations. We can use it to strengthen our own learning behaviors, making them into strong, reliable habits.

Remember the example from earlier in my life that I shared in the introduction: I was teaching failing fourth graders in a deprived neighborhood to read. Because I was new at this special after-hours school, I was assigned the four least capable, most distractible students, who were unable to accommodate to a normal classroom.

When one student did a good job at paying attention, at first I would immediately give him or her a whole M&M. Then gradually I would give M&Ms less and less frequently and would even cut the candy in half in front of the student and give her/him one half and myself the other half. That process would make us both smile and laugh, and that — having fun as we were learning — was as much a reinforcer as the small piece of candy.

Using these small reinforcers worked well with my four students. They began to excel. A couple of other volunteer teachers were assigned to imitate my methods.

An interesting wrinkle cropped up at this point, though. Many of our students had had no breakfast. And the new teachers gave as "rewards" to their students large, one-inch cubes of sweet, gooey candy. One alone would begin to make these little kids ill on their empty stomachs. Of course, they had no desire for another "reward," and their learning behaviors reflected that.

We learned a very important lesson: contrary to what intuition may tell you, small rewards work best when it comes to reinforcing behavior. The purpose: instill a drive for more, attaching the want for more to the will to learn.

Regular reinforcements in the beginning and intermittent reinforcements after a habit begins to form work best.

Self-reinforcement, using these guidelines, may be the most powerful tool you will have for strengthening your Motivation, for increasing your intelligence and for developing reliable and sustainable learning habits.

Here's an example of using self-reinforcement: A psychology Ph.D. student at Stanford was having trouble writing his dissertation. He decided to use a novel self-reinforcement — he posted on his office door the progress he'd make each day (or the lack of it), inviting passersby to applaud or boo. I was told he finished in record time and, last I heard, he was a highly respected professor and researcher at the University of Pennsylvania.

You can learn more about an optimum variety and scheduling of reinforcements in Skinner's books and on the Internet.

Exercise
What are effective reinforcements for you?
How would you use these reinforcers to strengthen specific learning activities and to convert them into reliable habits?
Write your answers in your notebook.

6) Chunking

A powerful approach to Motivation is a technique called "chunking." This involves dividing a difficult challenge into small, easily accomplished steps. When the helpless child within us looks at a large task, it may seem overwhelming and impossible, causing us anxiety. Yet, when you break the task down into a number of small steps and put your focus on just that one next, small, readily accomplished goal, your confidence in success is magnified and your Motivation is greatly empowered.

7) Behavior affects motivation

William James, considered the father of American psychology, said. "Smile and you will feel happy."

Try it right now. Put this book down, smile and see how it makes you feel.

Now, firm your lips and frown a bit. Did you find yourself feeling slightly more determined?

Next, imagine yourself taking a break and going on a brisk walk. Did you feel an increase in energy?

Practice makes perfect. You may practice using these simple methods to generate first an initial and then a strong and sustained Motivation to improve your intelligence, and for other specific accomplishments.

8) Self-Perception

Self-perception also greatly affects Motivation.

One of the most effective tools to support your quest for a high-level learning ability is to be able to picture yourself as a high-level learner. Having a positive self-perception helps boost your Motivation. If we practice seeing ourselves as an interested, accomplished learner, our behaviors will begin to approximate those activities in reality.

So, several times each day in front of the mirror, rehearse seeing yourself as an active, successful learner, and then as you successfully begin to imitate that image in reality, feel it, enjoy it, and consider reinforcing yourself.

A caution on self-image: When rehearsing a positive self-image, be aware that it is a goal and not a current reality. It's best to generate a modest, rather than intense, urge to achieve your desired reality. An intensely needed self-image, one that is far from reality, can produce a chronic, destructive anxiety.

Exercise

What self-images would doom your Motivation to learn?
What self-images would support your Motivation to learn?
Do you think it's possible to control or modify our self-image?
(Write your answers in your notebook.)

Now rehearse:
First see yourself in one of your habitual negative images
(only if you have them).
Then replace it with a positive image of yourself.
Repeat four times. Be patient and persistent. Sometimes
it takes awhile.
Now imagine yourself enjoying and benefitting from learning.
Imitating that image will spur you into consistently productive and
enjoyable learning behaviors.

Rehearse this positive image several times each day. For many of us, this one easy activity will prove most effective in producing a high-powered learner. Try it at night before bedtime in order to let it gradually be absorbed over time by your subconscious.

9) Perception of the outside world
When we see our world as an oppressive, threatening place, when we see our learning goal as one that is impossible to achieve, learning feels as though it is a hopeless and worthless endeavor.

On the other hand, when we focus on the half-full glass and when we work diligently and in small steps, we are very likely to succeed.

Perceptions and conceptions will be covered at greater length in the chapter on Concept Formation.

10) Attitude
Attitude may be the commander-in-chief of motivators.

Having a positive attitude about learning — and about the process of improving your learning skills — can greatly enhance your ability to learn and your enjoyment of learning.

Exercise
What attitudes do you have that may interfere with learning?
What attitudes do you have that support and encourage learning?
(Write your answers in your notebook.)

Now, take a moment to imagine shifting from one of your negative attitudes to one of your positive attitudes. Practice feeling and seeing yourself with that positive attitude for a few moments, and then practice that several times a day until, in a couple of months, it feels like a natural and permanent part of your personality to be a motivated learner.

Especially in the beginning, pick learning challenges that invite success — starting with very simple ones, then moving on gradually to ones that are slightly more difficult and complex. Pay attention to and remember — and enjoy — your successes. Let them propel you to slightly greater ones.

11) Task perception

When you see a task as huge and impossible to achieve (or yourself as punished for doing it), in all likelihood you will be guaranteed of failure.

Instead, when you break a task into smaller pieces, and perceive the part of the task you are taking on as achievable and yourself as succeeding and enjoying the benefits from it, the probability of success will be multiplied.

Focus primarily just on the next small, simple part of the task that you will accomplish next. Practice seeing yourself succeeding at that specific piece of the task, and at the same time, practice seeing yourself enjoying this learning process and benefitting from it.

12) Prioritizing

Prioritizing is as crucial to Motivation and intelligence building as perceptions, reinforcement, behavior habits and attitudes.

If I review my options and make a decision that today, for this hour, a particular task is the most important thing for me to do, chances of me getting done are far greater than if I leave it to a haphazard "maybe" or "possibly," or even as a non-prioritized equal among other tasks on my daily list.

So, say you've decided to build your intelligence. You've made the commitment and set aside specific times and days to work at it. Be sure that during those times, improving your intelligence is the very highest priority for you, and then set about succeeding at it.

13) Self-talk
We will address self-talk under the Communications chapter. For now, be mindful of the way we continuously address ourselves subliminally with self-talk. Become aware of both your negative and positive self-talk. Work to dilute negatives and replace them with positives.

SUMMARY

Motivation is the fulcrum upon which this whole Skilligence Framework rests. Intelligence development depends to some small degree on wishing for it. But much more, it depends on will — on a regular, insistent, focused, habitual will to improve it.

Remember, development of each of the other nine skill components of intelligence — from Relaxation and Attention to Precision Learning — depends on the development and entrenchment of your reliable, dependable Motivation, that persistent determination to learn.

Consciously and regularly strengthen your Motivation to increase your intelligence by the following simple steps:

1) Identify the precise benefits you will reap from a more powerful learning ability, including the pleasure of seeing yourself as a more intelligent person.

2) Keep an image of those benefits clearly in your mind. Remind yourself of them at least once every single day.

3) Decide how much of your time you are able to and will allot to this program. Even a small amount of regular, well-designed work will make a large difference.

4) Make a commitment now to stick to your action plan, which you will learn to design in the Precision Learning chapter.

5) Regularly picture yourself carrying out and completing this action plan and enjoying the fruits of this successful labor — that is, your own gradually expanding learning power.

The degree to which you decide to adhere to the above five-step protocol will likely determine just how successful the Skilligence Framework will be for you.

With all that you now know about Motivation, increasing it is usually relatively simple. The explanation is a little complex, but carrying it out proves to be far less complicated.

Helpful hints
1) Practice feeling focused and determined. Then, each evening, narrow your Motivation down to just what it is you wish to accomplish the next day.

When you hear yourself say, "I can't," respond, "I can! I can! I will!"

2) As you go about your week and before you progress on to the next chapter, remember:

Motivation gets you started; habit keeps you going.

So the key is to motivate yourself to build the learning habit.

SKILLIGENCE'S
Seven-Step
MOTIVATION-BUILDING
approach:

1. Every day, rehearse in the mirror, telling yourself you are a competent, happily motivated, goal-oriented person. See yourself walking in beauty and accomplishing your goals easily.

2. Practice feeling clear-headed and happily motivated as you schedule and accomplish several simple tasks.

3. Divide slightly larger tasks into smaller, simpler tasks, and then feel motivated as you accomplish each part.

4. Pat yourself on the back and reward yourself when you succeed in feeling motivated and as you accomplish small parts of increasingly larger, more complex tasks.

5. Keep a journal about negative motivations you sometimes feel; then rehearse replacing them with positive ones.

6. Keep your goal in mind at all times.

7. Chunk, chunk, chunk.

And, finally, when your skill with Motivation is reliable, focus a powerful Motivation-to-learn on building the other nine component skills of intelligence. Then, using all of those powerful learning skills, focus on your most important long-term goal.

ADDENDA: For those with already medium or high-level Motivation, pick just one of the dimensions to develop further. Read about it. Coach yourself daily.

For those still with low-level Motivation, review Attention and Relaxation; chunk the current step toward your goal into tinier steps; remind yourself to focus solely on the next, tiny, easy step, and accomplish it. Attend to and reward yourself modestly for that small success. You are your own coach.

Coach yourself daily.

REFERENCES & RESOURCES

Alberti, Robert, Ph.D. & Emmons, Michael, Ph.D. *Your Perfect Right: Assertivemess and Equality in your Life and Relationships*. Atascadero, Ca: Impact Publishers, 2001.

Buckingham, J. *Coping with Criticism*. Logos International, 1978.

Candland, Douglas K., editor. *Emotion: Bodily Change*. New York, NY: Van Nostrand, 2003.

Colvin, Geoff. *Talent Is Overrated: What really separates world-class performers from everyone else*. New York, NY: Portfolio Trade, 2010.

Curtin, M.E. *Symposium on Love*. Behavioral Publications, 1973.

Dobson, J. *Dare to Discipline*. Carol Stream, il: Tyndale House, 1970.

Duhigg, C. *The Power of Habit*. New York, NY: Random House, 2012.

Fromm, E. *The Art of Loving*. New York, NY: Harper & Row, 1966.

Gendlin, Eugene T. *Focusing*. New York, NY: Bantam, 1982.

Gaylin, W., M.D. *The Rage Within, Anger in Modern Life*. New York, NY: Simon & Schuster, 1984.

Harvard Medical School Special Health Report. "Positive Psychology." 2016.

Hutschnecker, Arnold, M.D. *The Will to Live*. New York: Simon & Schuster, 1983.

Laing, R.D. *Knots*. New York, NY: Pantheon, 1970.

McClelland, D.C. *Motives, Personality, and Society, Selected Papers*. Santa Barbara, Ca: Praeger Publishers, 1984.

Morgenbesser, S. & Walsh, J. *Free Will*. Upper Saddle River, NJ: Prentice Hall, 1962.

Murray, E.J. *Motivation and Emotion*. Upper Saddle River, NJ: Prentice Hall, 1964.

Neill, A.S. *Freedom — Not License!* New York, NY: Hart Publishing Co., 1966.

Pink, Daniel H. *Drive: The surprising truth about what motivates us.* New York, NY: Riverhead Books, 2011.

Richo, David. *When the Past Is Present: Healing the emotional wounds that sabotage our relationships.* Boston, Ma.: Shambhala Publications, 2008.

Seligman, Martin, Ph.D. *Learned Optimism: How to change your mind and your life.* New York, NY: Vintage, 2006.

Stutz, P. & Michels, B. *The Tools: 5 tools to help you find courage, creativity, and willpower.* New York, NY: Random House, 2012.

Teevan, R.C. & Birney, R.C. Theories of Motivation in Learning. New York, NY: Van Nostrand, 1964.

Waitley, D. & Witt, R,l. *The Joy of Working.* New York, NY: Dodd, Mead & Co., 1985.

"Memory is, without a doubt, the most powerful (and practical) tool of everyday life. By linking both your past and your future, memory gives you the power to plan, to reason, to perceive and to understand. As long as thinking and insight are important in how we live our lives, memory will be critical as well. The better your memory, the more information you'll have at your immediate disposal and the better your thinking will be."
—Peter M. Vishton, associate professor in psychology at William & Mary College, in *Scientific Secrets for a Powerful Memory*.

CHAPTER FIVE

SKILL 4: MEMORY

Think about it — how could we accomplish even the simplest daily chores if we fail to remember them?

With a good memory, we have access to more information with which we can better understand ourselves and the world we live in, as well as solve important problems and create and accomplish things.

In fact, the success of all educational efforts is completely dependent upon the complex of processes that make up memory. "Memory" is a broad term — it includes learning, retaining, recalling, recognizing and relearning.

When you understand memory — its varied dimensions, its huge improvability and the processes that contribute to that improvability — you will be on the road to improving your own memory.

Review exercise

It's a good idea to review the previous chapters, Relaxation, Attention and Motivation, as all are prerequisites of Memory.

What do you remember that seemed important to you about:

· Relaxation and intelligence?
· Attention and learning ability?
· Motivation and intelligence?

(Write your answers in your notebook.)

Exercise

Now, switching to the current topic of Memory, list as many things as you can think of that are important for you to remember. (For example, your phone number, your address, etc.)

MEMORY PROCESSING

Memory is, essentially, the ability to store and retrieve information. There are three overarching processes involved with memory: 1) the inputting of information, referred to as "encoding," 2) storage, or retaining, and 3) retrieval, or recall.

Much inputting takes place without us really thinking about it. Consider, for example, where and with whom you had lunch yesterday. It's not hard to remember that information, even though you didn't work at remembering it. But there's a lot of information — such as that in school textbooks — that we have to work at inputting, or encoding, into our brain.

There are different ways to process information into memory. Among them are "rote" and "meaningful" learning.

"Rote" learning is when you memorize something without necessarily understanding it. It often involves repeating, or rehearsing, information until you do remember it.

The technique called "chunking" is quite useful in rote learning. Covered also in the Motivation chapter, chunking is when you break a task down into smaller, more easily accomplished steps.

Suppose, for example, you're trying to remember this string of 12 numbers: 437890530574

Rather than trying to remember them all together in one string, it's easier to remember them in groups of four numbers each: 4378 9053 0574

Interestingly, telephone numbers are divided and separated for just this reason — because it's easier to remember smaller bits of information.

"Meaningful" learning is when you learn new information by relating it to prior, relevant knowledge — that is, you anchor that new information in something you already know and understand.

As an example, if you want to remember the countries of the world, start with a few at a time, and remember them as part of a particular geographic region. (This utilizes both meaningful learning and chunking.)

If, say, you're trying to memorize the countries that make up the Middle East, start by picturing the Arabian Peninsula and understand that it is in Southwest Asia, linked to Africa via Egypt. Although Egypt spans two continents with most of it geographically in North Africa, it is often considered to be politically part of the Middle East.

The Arabian Peninsula is bordered by the Persian Gulf in the west, the Arabian Sea to its south, and the Red Sea to its east.

With meaningful learning, a student can use existing relevant knowledge — in this case that of the location of North Africa and Southwest Asia — to understand new concepts and facilitate new learning.

GETTING STARTED

In order to get started on improving your memory, choose to work on just one of the several memory sub-skills and tools you will learn about below. It is less critical which you choose than it is to just go ahead and choose one.

Once you begin to see small bits of progress, it will be powerful motivation for future efforts to develop each sub-skill.

But before we move on to the tools below, remember to follow these four tips while you're using the tools below to improve your memory:

Relax: Quiet yourself. Envision a calm lake. Then envision yourself as that calm lake. Identify the source of any anxiety present and relax it away. Focus on the calm lake.

Focus & mindfulness: To begin inputting information into your memory, focus precisely, clearly and vividly on what you want to remember.

Make it important: Repeat the information you are working on remembering. Tell yourself that it is important for you to remember this, and say why.

Review, review, review: Now review what you just memorized and repeat it again several times.

Memory tools & sub-skills
Here are brief descriptions of several useful memory tools. Later in this chapter we will delve more in depth into a few of them.

Chunking: As discussed earlier in this chapter, chunking — breaking a task down into smaller, easily achievable steps — is a simple but powerful tool. When you use it for memory improvement, you can memorize three or four bits of information at a time, and then combine those bits into slightly larger groups and review.

≈≈≈≈≈

My success using chunking
Chunking worked great for me learning German words for the GRE in grad school. I did most of it on one plane trip. I had a thousand flash cards. I already knew some of the words. I would take three or four at a time and memorize them.

Then I'd review two packs of them. When I remembered them, I learned another two packs of three or four each and when I'd learned them and reviewed them, I then reviewed the four packs together and so on and passed the GRE in record time. This despite the fact that as a child, and after suffering two head injuries during World War II, my memory was very poor. After training at age 40, my memory became far better than average.

≈≈≈≈≈

The Tree: This is an excellent tool for schoolwork, for example for remembering the concepts in a book. To get started, draw a skeleton tree. Write on the trunk the name and subject of the book. Then draw the main limbs for each chapter. Next, draw twigs to represent ideas and important details in each chapter. Later, make a separate tree for each important chapter.

Vivid Association:
Another method for remembering a list of items is to link vivid and, sometimes, absurd associations between each. The more absurd, the more colorful and vivid, the easier and more readily you'll remember them. (More on vivid association later in this chapter.) This tool seems to work well with almost anything. Early on, even with a very poor memory, I once remembered 50 random words using this tool.

The House: Use this technique to remember a list of words, like a shopping list or a group of muscles for your anatomy class, by putting a different item in a specific place in the rooms of your imagined home. As you imagine walking through the house, practice seeing a different item clearly and vividly in each place (sofa, TV, chair, fridge, counter). This tool was developed and widely used by Ancient Roman orators in order to remember their speeches.

Practice: Whichever memory tools work best for you, practice using them regularly. For example, try practicing with auto license plate numbers. After just a glance, first remember just the last three numbers, then, when that gets easy, the whole license number, then, when that is easy, the whole number with the last three numbers of the next license you see, then two entire license plate numbers. With this type of practice, it will keep getting easier and a little faster. (Note: This kind of practice strengthens Attention, which strengthens immediate memory.)

Teach It, Write It: Teaching a subject is a great way to learn it. In fact, there's even a name for it — scientists refer to it as "the protégé effect". Students tapped to teach their fellow classmates, or those who tutor younger children, were found to score higher on tests than those who were learning solely for themselves.

Writing notes can also help people remember information, including anything from a shopping list to a class lecture. (Interestingly, some studies have found that handwriting notes during a class lecture improves recall better than taking notes on a laptop.)

Identify, Record and Reinforce Progress: Success begets success. Reinforce your progress, no matter how small, as this will help you continue to improve your skills. (More on this in the chapter on Precision Learning.) Always practice easy challenges first, then slowly, only with successes on the easy ones, move on to slightly more difficult challenges.

Organize: Organize material on index cards, calendars, in file folders and/or on the computer. Figure out which method of organizing works for you. As an example, if you are working on learning countries in a particular geographic area, use separate cards for each area, like one for Eastern Europe, another for Central Europe; similarly you would divide Africa and South America into parts. (This would involve chunking, associating and organizing.)

It will also be helpful to look up "organizing tips" on the Internet for more suggestions.

A few exercises to try
The three tools that helped me the most through graduate school were The Tree, The Word System and Vivid Association. Below, these three and a few others are explored in a little greater detail.

The Tree
Start by drawing a simple tree with several branches on a piece of paper.

Next, write the title of a textbook you are currently studying on the trunk.

Then, write the name of each chapter on the branches, one chapter title per branch. Add more branches to your tree if you need to.

Now, skim through the first chapter of the textbook you've chosen, add twigs to its branch, and write a couple of notes on the twigs to remind you of the key points in that chapter.

You would then do the same for the remaining chapters. An important chapter would get its own tree.

Previewing them in this way creates a framework onto which your subsequent reading and learning will attach.

In addition, if you own the textbook, underline and mark an asterisk on important passages as you read, partly to impress it on your memory, but also to facilitate review.

The Word System
Suppose you're off to the hardware store and you need five items: An ax, a rake, a saw, light bulbs and nails. See if you can rearrange the items on your shopping list so the first letters form a word.

Example:
Saw
Nails
Ax
Rake
Light bulbs

SNARL!

If you say the word "snarl" to yourself when you enter the hardware store, you'll more than likely recall the five items on the list.

With some modest practice, you can extend the remembered list to a dozen items — and even more with a little additional practice.

Vivid Associations: The Link System

Another method for remembering a list of items is to link vivid and, if possible, absurd associations between each. Make vivid associations, some absurd, to tie them together. The more absurd, the more colorful and vivid, the easier and more readily you'll remember them.

Start with a small list of random words; then do the same with slightly longer lists.

For example, you might associate the ax with a scary scene from a horror movie. The rake may bring up vivid memories of bonfires of fallen leaves when you were a child. Create an image or story that will link each of the vivid associations.

With practice you will remember long lists of far more items than just five. When I was practicing it, as I've mentioned previously, one time I remembered 50 items, and competitors can remember multiples of that.

The House

This system was developed and used by Ancient Roman orators in order to remember their long speeches.

Using our shopping list for the hardware store once again, I'll picture my own house, which will be similar to many: the living room with a recliner, a TV, a couch and a wall with a painting on it, and the kitchen with a dishwasher, a fridge, a stove and a sink.

After placing each of the five items throughout the house, I would walk through the rooms and rehearse remembering the five items and have some confidence that when I got to the store, they would be recallable.

A FEW MORE TIPS & TRICKS

Looking back

For everyday events, Looking back is a most useful tool. It is by far my favorite. I use it constantly. Even when I was much younger, I used to panic when I'd forget where I parked my car in a large mall parking area or at the movies, or which locker I used at the pool. Now, at over 90 years old, as I walk away from my car or my locker, I make a point to look back twice at the car or the locker, like snapping a picture twice. Miracle of miracles, when I am finished with my shopping or my workout, without thinking or wondering about it again, I just automatically go right to where my car or locker is.

Remembering names

If you have trouble remembering names, here are simple suggestions that are likely to be helpful:

Repeat the name right away and listen to yourself. You might let it sound like a clarifying question. And, as you do, look at and see the person clearly, twice.

Notice details of the face: shape of head, color of hair and eyes, etc. Then repeat the name a couple of times to yourself, visualizing the person each time as you do, and exaggerate some facet of his/her face or appearance.

Mindfulness

Mindfulness may be the single most powerful aid to memory, while its absence the greatest dissolver of memory. One key to achieving a reliable memory, therefore, may be practicing and reinforcing increasing your mindfulness — that is, attending clearly, fully and solely to what is going on.

Staying Healthy Helps Memory

Remember what the medical community advises for strengthening both attention and memory: eat healthy; exercise regularly; get adequate rest. They do make a difference.

Here, also, are several memory-boosting tips and tricks from the Harvard Medical School:

1. Follow routines, such as leaving your car keys, glasses and cell phone in the same place every day so that finding them becomes a "no brainer."

2. Slow down and pay attention to what you are doing to give your brain's memory systems enough time to create an enduring memory.

3. Avoid distracting or noisy environments and multitasking — the major memory busters in today's fast-paced society.

4. Get enough sleep, reduce stress, and check with your doctor to see if any of your medications affect memory — all potential memory spoilers.

These tips apply as well to Attention and all the core and higher skills.

Exercise
(Write your ideas in your notebook.)
What can you do to support the development of each facet of memory?
Remember, regular practice with almost any memory task will increase your Memory skill.

For additional reading
Two of the very best books on building a powerful memory are *The Memory Book,* by Harry Lorayne and Jerry Lucas, and *How to Develop a Brilliant Memory Week by Week,* by Dominic O'Brien. The latter is the most recent and is written by an eight-times World Memory champion, whereas *The Memory Book* is almost a timeless classic. Either will give you several exercises that will fit your needs for building a better memory.

CONCLUSION

Memory is a critical component of intelligence and it is hugely improvable. Some educators argue that we shouldn't put effort into building memory. We should, instead, emphasize understanding and creativity.

To that I would say that all three are necessary, and memory is key to improving the others.

With a good memory, we get a lot of information with which we can better understand ourselves and the world we live in, as well as solve important problems, create, accomplish, relate well and live comfortably.

And with a good memory, we can build a good vocabulary. This, in turn, leads to good communication, which in turn, we will learn, leads to almost every other important goal we may have.

Especially regarding innovation and creativity: the more varied items we can pull from our memory, the more innovative and creative we may be.

REFERENCES & RESOURCES

Fabiny, Anne, M.D., Harvard Medical School Special Health Report. "Improving Memory."

Higbee, Kenneth L. *Your Memory: How It Works and How to Improve It*. Upper Saddle River, N.J.: Prentice Hall, 1977.

Houston, John P. *Fundamentals of Learning and Memory*. San Diego, Calif.: Harcourt Brace Jovanovich, 1986.

Lorayne, Harry & Lucas, Jerry. *The Memory Book*. New York, N.Y.: Ballantine, 1974.

McLeod, S. A. (2007). *Stages of Memory — Encoding Storage and Retrieval*. Retrieved from www.simplypsychology.org/memory.html

O'Brien, Dominic. *How to Develop a Brilliant Memory Week by Week*. London, U.K.: Duncan Baird, 2005.

SparkNotes Editors. "SparkNote on Memory." SparkNotes.com. SparkNotes LLC. 2005. Web. 26 Mar. 2017.

Vishton, Peter M. *Scientific Secrets for a Powerful Memory*. Chantilly, Va.: The Great Courses.

Internet Resources
Coursera: www.coursera.org
Edgenuity: www.edgenuity.com
Kaplan University Online: www.kaplanuniversity.edu
Lumosity: www.lumosity.com Improve memory with scientifically designed brain exercises.
Mind Tools: www.mindtools.com
Silva Life System: www.SilvalifeSystem.com/Memory

NOTE: Check in also with your local community college. While Relaxation, Attention and Motivation may not be taught in your local community college or university learning center, Memory is likely to be.

CHAPTER SIX

SKILL 5: COMMUNICATIONS

Communications is at the very core of intelligence. Merriam-Webster Dictionary says "communications" is, essentially, a technique for expressing ideas effectively.

The ability to communicate effectively encompasses all dimensions of Communications, including reading, writing, listening and speaking.

According to an article in the Harvard Business Review (Feb. 4, 2013, Zenger and Folkman), Communications skills are what distinguish good leaders from poor leaders. Further, not only are good Communications skills key to career advancement, they are also the key to better relationships, to better learning, and to a more enjoyable overall life.

This chapter will deal at least a bit with each of the dimensions of communications, including vocabulary, body language and talking to yourself, also referred to as "self-talk".

Exercise 1
Consider the following: Do you communicate differently with your parents, spouse, child, teacher, student, colleague, boss, employee, buddy?
Consider not only your words, but your manner, attitude and content.
(Write your thoughts in your notebook.)

Exercise 2
How do better Relaxation, Attention, Motivation and/or Memory skills help build our Communications skills and our overall ability to learn?
(Write your answers in your notebook.)

BUILDING COMMUNICATIONS SKILLS
To start, here are nine facets of Communications and suggestions for things you can do to improve your skills:

Vocabulary
- List and use in a sentence three new words each day.
- Have a good dictionary handy.
- Read and write every day.

Reading
- Read easy material quickly each day; write a quick summary.
- Count the words every third day. Graph progress.
- Take a speed-reading course.

Writing
- Take a course in typing.
- Write simple material every day. Read it aloud.
- Take a writing course and/or join a local writing group.
- Write a daily journal.
- Build both physical and mental writing skills.

Speaking
- Practice expressing your feelings.
- Join a Toastmasters group.
- Read aloud simple material daily for a few minutes.
   —Every third time, record it and listen.
   —Rate and make notes as your clarity, timing and variety of content improve.

Questioning
Practice asking questions, using trial-and-error, in order to get more comfortable and better at it.

Listening
Read about and join a group to learn "active listening."

Body language
Monitor your body language and modify it to say what you want it to say.

Language of love
Read *The Five Love Languages*, by Gary Chapman, to become more supportive and affectionate.

Self-talk
Monitor it and encourage positives.

EXPLORING FURTHER
Now, we will focus more in-depth on four of those facets: Reading, Writing, Speaking and Listening.

READING

Of all the communications skills, improving your reading skill will be of utmost importance for anyone considering a return to school. So, unless you already have a high level of reading skill, it's a good idea to take a course in speed-reading. In a relatively short time, you will become both a faster reader and have greater comprehension and retention.

≈≈≈≈≈

"Much is known about reading for effective learning which includes a composite of special skills beyond those commonly labeled basic reading skills. Among these are: 1. Locating information, 2. Organizing information and 3. Planning for its retention."
— Smith & Dechant (1961)

≈≈≈≈≈

Reading rate

The rate at which you read is greatly improvable. But interestingly, if no effort is made to increase reading rate, improvement stops by about the sixth grade.

Numerous studies have indicated that not only can reading rate be increased, comprehension also rises when you learn rapid-reading techniques.

Although many studies use speed-reading machines to track a students' reading rate progress, one study reported steady improvement of students' reading rate by simply using 50 ten-minute sessions over the course of a school year with students just reading easy material as rapidly as possible for one minute and then counting the words.

A good reading and comprehension skills program will multiply these effects many times.

To get you started on improving the rate of your reading, here is a brief introduction to speed-reading:

Speed-reading exercise

To complete this exercise, you'll need a timer and a book that you've not read before.

First, read for one minute and count the words.

(An easy way to count words: First, count the lines, then the number of words in a random three lines. Average those three lines. Then, multiply the average words per line by the number of lines.)

Then, relax your hands and your eyes, your jaw and tongue and throat. This is to reduce, and then eliminate, sub-vocalizing. Sub-vocalizing is when you say the words in your head while you're reading. And it causes you to read at the same rate that you speak, slowing you down.

Once you've relaxed your hands, eyes, jaw, tongue and throat, open the book to the first page of a new section. With a relaxed hand, guide your eyes by moving your fingers under the line of type gradually faster for one minute. Write down the number of words you read.

Next, try that again for one minute. Again, count the words.

Try that a third time. Again, count the words.

Did you make some improvement with this short practice?

Normal progress with continued practice will be to, very gradually, have the hand first move under the lines across the page slowly and then gradually faster. Then after much practice, the hand will just move down the page and, finally, for simple reading material, just turn the pages. This is likely to take weeks, possibly months, of training. But progress is very likely to include a multiplying of your present reading speed, as well as improved comprehension and enjoyment.

When finished reading, make a note summarizing with some detail first each paragraph, then each page, and then each section of what you've read, and finally, perhaps, a whole book or article. Use the "tree" concept that you learned in the Memory segment to summarize the content.

(More on comprehension in the Concept Formation chapter.)

≈≈≈≈≈

Reminder: *This book is not intended to offer adequate training in any of the 10 component skills of intelligence for significant and sustained gains to occur. Instead, this book is designed to introduce them in order to give you an understanding of their value along with ways to improve them. Then it is up to you.*

≈≈≈≈≈

*"The skill of writing is
to create a context in which
other people can think."*
—Edwin Schlossberg

*"The role of a writer is
not to say what we all can say,
but what we are unable to say."*
—Anais Nin

WRITING

The ability to articulate clearly in writing is fundamental to successful communications. To improve your writing ability, it's important to practice. Practice writing for at least a few minutes every day. It can be about anything — yourself, your family, the world, local events. Use a computer, a journal or a yellow legal pad — whatever works for you.

In the beginning, don't worry at all about editing for grammar or meaning. Just let it flow. The initial goal is to develop an easy fluency.

Also, remember to relax your arms, your hands and your fingers each time before you write or type so your writing muscles move easily.

As you develop your writing skills, also practice outlining in order to get a comprehensive, well-organized and smooth-flowing body of work. (This applies to both speaking and writing.)

Begin to organize your writing into beginning, body and end. Attend to one small part at a time. Keep writing easily and quickly, but be relaxed, optimistic, enthusiastic and unrushed.

Before you start, relax and quiet yourself for a minute in order to get a picture of what it is you are going to write and of yourself enjoying the process. Then let it flow.

As you progress, begin to read some of your written work over the next day and see where you can improve, where you can make it just a bit more simple, a bit more easily understood — and more expressive of what you really mean.

Keep a dictionary and thesaurus handy.

Remind yourself periodically that writing can be very frustrating— it can be hard to express in written words what you really mean. Learn to accept that you may need to revise a document, letter, report or story numerous times, without getting angry at yourself. If you do get frustrated, find an activity to dilute that feeling —for example, take a few minutes break to do an easy puzzle or take a short walk — in fact, schedule time for activities like that.

Learn to 'Keyboard'

In today's digital world, it's essential for everyone to have fast, 10-finger keyboarding skills. Many free tutorials are available online — do an online search for "keyboarding" or "learn to type."

≈≈≈≈≈

"To become a writer, you have to follow a few rules: Show, don't tell. Avoid clichés. Be specific. Try not to repeat yourself.
"These rules work for me whether I'm writing an essay like this or an ad at the agency where I work as a writer and creative director. I've learned that people don't love to be told things. But they don't mind being shown things. When you demonstrate an idea for a reader or viewer, you let him participate in the process.
"I try to teach this to the copywriters who work for me. Find the story. Make it matter. No one wants to be lectured to. And that's true if you're creating a mobile app, a TV spot or even a PowerPoint."
—Jim Sollisch
(Sollisch, a creative director and partner at an ad agency in Cleveland, Ohio, has had personal essays published in The New York Times, The Wall Street Journal and The Washington Post, and he's been a commentator for National Public Radio.)

≈≈≈≈≈

And, finally
Here's a final suggestion for developing a high-level writing skill: Once a week, research a subject of interest and write a paragraph or two about it.

PUBLIC SPEAKING
Improving your speaking ability — and more specifically, your public speaking ability — will help you in many areas of your life. For example, it will help you improve your overall communications skills, you'll get better at perceiving people's reaction to your message, and it will boost your self-confidence — and all of this will help you in both your career and relationships.

One way to become a better public speaker is to find a few friends who are interested in improving their public speaking too. When you get together, each of you bring a book or other written material. Then each participant reads a short passage from the material they brought and gets feedback from the others. Practice reading the same passage several times and make notes as to improvement.

Another useful exercise is to listen to good public speakers, either in-person, online, or on television, and make notes on effective techniques. Search for TED talks on the Internet and watch them for examples of excellent public speaking skills.

For additional help in public speaking, consider a local community college class and/or joining a local Toastmasters club. Toastmasters is a nonprofit organization that teaches public speaking via a network of local clubs.

Another way to improve your public speaking is to read different material aloud each day for just a few minutes. Record it and listen to yourself periodically to see how you sound. Then read it again, concentrating on becoming clearer, your pace more relaxed, your tone varied and energized, your words more distinct, your message more real.

At the beach, practice speaking out against the sound of the wind and the waves. The ancient orators did this to build their wind — their breathing power — and their power to project. And then do the same with a pebble or marble in your mouth to build clarity.

Speaking in Public Confidently

Here are a few tips to help prepare yourself for speaking confidently in public:

Tip 1: SEEK & GRAB opportunities for speaking. As a beginner, make a great number of small and successful speeches. It builds your confidence.

Tip 2: ACCEPT invitations to speak only on familiar subjects with sufficient time to prepare. Otherwise politely refuse. It is very good to speak on new subjects, but not foolishly, and not as a beginner.

Tip 3: PREPARE beforehand. But never ever prepare, think or worry about it at the venue. Always speak short, soft and sweet. People will like you.

Tip 4: REACH the venue before the program starts. Casually familiarize yourself with the hall, dais, podium, mike, organizers, staff, attendees, etc.

Tip 5: GREET the maximum number of people, circulate, make short introductions with new faces, smile at strangers, be cheerful.

Tip 6: RELAX yourself in the chair physically and mentally while awaiting your turn. Take a deep breath, make a short and secret meditation, mentally play your favorite sound track, feel friends cheering you up, or visualize a scene of past success. Then focus your full attention on what is going on in the meeting. Keep your chin up and eyes on the stage.

Tip 7: RISE slowly when your name is called, walk normally (not casually or lazily) up to the dais, confidently climb up, look at the people all around and smile and take a comfortable and confident stance.

Tip 8: GIVE a smooth salutation and introduction, and begin slowly. Within a few seconds you will feel in full command.

'I' MESSAGES

Here's a communications practice that can help you in relationships of any kind, whether with family, a spouse, with friends, or at work:

Sending so-called "I" messages rather than "you" messages is a good practice and can be of critical importance to working out issues.

"You" messages clamp blame on others. By using "I" messages, you take responsibility for your own feelings and reactions.

Example: "I felt hurt when I heard that" versus "You're a nasty person."

(See "Resources" at the end of this chapter for more on "I" versus "you" messages.)

LISTENING

Active, engaged listening is actually more difficult than speaking. It requires staying in the moment when you're listening to others. And it is a crucial component of Communications.

The extraordinary value of a great listening skill is illustrated by Robert Caro's description of Lyndon Johnson in his biography *Lyndon Johnson, The Passage of Power*. Johnson, as described by Caro, was the most talented United States politician of the postwar era, a peerless congressional dealmaker. Much of Johnson's unique power came from his unparalleled ability to listen. Johnson was not a great public speaker, but when he needed a crucial vote, he would focus persistently and exclusively on listening to his colleague or opponent until he learned what that politician needed. Then Johnson would trade what was needed for the politician's vote.

Active Listening is a Communications technique in which the listener paraphrases what they hear to make sure he or she understands what the other meant.

Emphasis should be on the feelings behind what is said, leaving time and space for corroboration or clarification.

Here are a few suggestions for improving your listening skills:
1) While listening to a lecture
   • Reflect to yourself what the lecturer is saying.
   • Remind yourself to be alert and interested. Re-attend frequently.
   • When taking notes, go over your notes as soon after class as possible — and then again periodically.

2) Get instruction in note-taking and organizing.

3) When listening to another individual

• Try active listening — reflecting the feelings and the meaning back to the person. It builds good relationships in family and in work.

This valuable skill takes practice. Try to improve it a little each time.

Exercise 1
You'll need a partner for this exercise in Active Listening.
· Take turns telling your partner about something that is important to you or something that happened yesterday or last week or last month.
· Do this for one minute.
· Then the partner will reflect on what he/she heard you say and the feelings they perceived. Do this for one minute.
· The speaker either corroborates the partner's perception or clarifies it further.
· Then switch and do the same in the other direction.

When you're finished, ask yourself:
How well did you reflect?
How comfortable were you at reflecting?
How did it feel to be listened to?
(Write your responses in your notebook.)

Exercise 2
Which Communication Skills might contribute most to developing your learning abilities?
How will you build your Communications Skills?
(Write responses in your notebook.)

Also consider:
- Practicing monitoring and listening to your own reactions.
- Listening to nature.
- Investigating Active Listening and "I" messages further. Perhaps join a group. These two skills alone will help you understand and relate warmly and supportively with your friends, spouse, children, family and coworkers.

CONCLUSION

The four key Communications skills — Reading, Writing, Speaking and Listening — are at the core of intelligence. Interestingly, using and developing these communication sub-skills requires the four basic components of intelligence: Relaxation, Attention, Motivation and Memory. In turn, all four are necessary for the use and improvement of each of the five higher-order components of intelligence: Computations, Concept Formation, Problem Solving, Creativity and Precision Learning.

Each of the Communications skills is hugely and readily improvable and as each improves, intelligence tends to surge right along with them.

All of the Communications sub-skills are taught well and in more detail at local schools and online, so you can continue your research and practice on your own.

Of course, the purpose of communicating is to give and get information and understanding, and that will be covered more in Chapter 7, Concept Formation. In the meantime, remind yourself that the better your Communications skills, the better will be your giving and getting of information and understanding.

REFERENCES & RESOURCES
Reading
Denby, David. *Great Books*. New York, NY: Simon and Schuster, 1996.

DeVine, C. Maury, Dissel, Claudia M., & Parrish, Kim D., Editors. *The Harvard Guide to Influential Books*.

Fadiman, Clifton. *The Lifetime Reading Plan*. New York, NY: Harper & Row, 1988.

Frank, Stanley D. Ed.D. *Remember Everything You Read*. New York, NY: Avon, 1990.

Kump, Peter. *Breakthrough Rapid Reading*. Upper Saddle River, NJ: Prentice Hall, 1999. New York, NY: Harper & Row, 1986.

Writing
Bosse, Nancy & Swenson, Elizabeth, Editors. *Grammar*. Greensboro, NC:

Carson-Dellosa, 2011. *The Foundation Center's Guide to Proposal Writing*. New York, NY: The Foundation Center, 2004.

Jackman, Ian, Editor. *The Writer's Mentor*. New York, NY: Random House, 2004.

Plotnik, Arthur. *The Elements of Editing: A Modern Guide for Editors and Journalists*. New York, NY: Collier, 1982.

Sollisch, Jim. *The Art of Repetition*, NY Times, May 13, 2013.

Strunk, William Jr. & White, E.B. *The Elements of Style*. London, U.K.: Longman, 1999.

Zinsser, William. *On Writing Well*. New York, NY: Harper Collins, 1994.

Speaking
Amram, Fred. M., & Benson, Frank T. *Creating a Speech, A Student's Workbook*. New York, NY: Scribner's, 1968.

Goodman, Gerald, Ph.D., & Esterly, Glenn. *The Talk Book: The Intimate Science of Communicating in Close Relationships*. Emmaus, PA: Rodale Press, 1988.

Donovan, Jeremey & Avery, Ryan. *Speaker Leader Champion*. New York, NY: McGraw Hill, 2014.

Lee, Irving, J. *How to Talk With People.* New York, NY: Harper & Brothers, 1952.

Rosenberg, Marshall B., Ph.D. *Nonviolent Communication: A Language of Compassion.* Encinitas, CA: PuddleDancer Press. 2000.

Safire, William. *Lend Me Your Ears: Great Speeches in History.* New York, NY: Norton, 2004.

Toastmasters: www.toastmasters.org

Listening

Bolton, Robert, Ph.D. *People Skills: How to Assert Yourself, Listen to Others, and Resolve Conflicts.* Upper Saddle River, NJ: Prentice Hall, 1979.

Gordon, Thomas. *Leader Effectiveness Training.* New York, NY: Wyden, 1977. Montgomery, Robert. *Listening Made Easy.* New York, NY: Amacom, 1981.

CHAPTER SEVEN

SKILL 6: COMPUTATIONS

Many people enjoy computations. For those fortunate folks, math is a pleasant game. But there are many, many more who are fearful and even phobic of math. For them, it is at the very least an unpleasant chore. In fact, because of that fear, a large number of careers are completely blocked for certain individuals.

With your newly developed Relaxation, Attention and chunking skills, math can become a pleasant game for you, too — if you start simple.

Success in many important areas of our everyday lives depends upon a facility with the several Computations processes.

For example: Which mortgage or auto loan is best? How much can we afford to pay for a house or a car? How many children should we have? How much should we allot for our vacation, for our medical and other insurance, for recreation, for education, for furniture and clothing? Which is a better financial move, renting or buying a home? How much, and in what, should we invest in order to assure a comfortable retirement?

Many careers require expertise in such math-dependent disciplines as finance, probability and statistics for success. Careers that require a high level of competence with math include medicine, securities analysis, computers, engineering, architecture, manufacturing — even auto repair and construction require computation skills.

Fear of math and serious math deficits can cut one's options down considerably in our increasingly demanding and complex modern world.

But it doesn't have to. And it shouldn't.

For if one relaxes and takes it slow and easy, building familiarity and competence in small steps from the bottom up, then the concepts and skills of the various levels of mathematics become more easily acquired.

Best of all, with these newly acquired skills a world of new opportunities opens up.

The purpose of this chapter is to give you a brief introduction to the several disciplines of Computations, so that when you decide to study them, you will have an initial familiarity and comfort with them.

NOTE: In this chapter, we will arbitrarily use "math" and "computations" interchangeably, as synonyms, though strictly speaking they are usually defined somewhat differently.

Four critical things to remember in regard to Computations:

1. Most important: In addition to being in sixth place in the Skilligence hierarchy, Computations is in itself a hierarchy of sub-skills. Facility at basic levels within the Computations hierarchy ensures progress at each next higher level.

2. Also important to remember is that development of the five prerequisite skills in the Skilligence hierarchy — Relaxation through Communications — assures development of the Computations skills.

3. Automaticity in math basics is usually necessary for facility in the more advanced math processes. "Automaticity" is the ability to do something without really thinking about it — allowing the skill or task to become an automatic habit, like, say, driving. It is usually the result of learning, repetition and practice.

More than that, if you are returning to school to study sciences and/or math, developing automaticity with flash cards, as described below, will ease and assure your successful progress.

4. Estimating allows approximating, which is often good enough.

BUILDING THE BASICS
So, to begin this process of building your capability with Computations skills, this chapter will: 1) Provide an overview of a number of common disciplines that require math skill; 2) Provide exercises in the more basic levels of math; and 3) Refer to sources for further instruction.

Begin by taking a look at the "Computations Includes" chart at the end of this chapter. Now, in order to begin to develop automaticity with the basics — that is, adding, subtracting, multiplying and dividing — you'll need a pack of 3 x 5 cards. Make two sets of cards, numbering them one through 12. Now, shuffle them and divide them into two packs, face down.

Then, turn up one card from each pack, add them and put them back down in a single pack.

After you're done with the piles of cards, do the same with multiplication, subtraction and division.

If you continue to practice with the cards, you should find that facility with the basics of adding, subtracting, multiplying and dividing is easy to build — and very worth a few minutes a day.

In order to build familiarity and comfort with numbers, I recommend working with these cards for at least a few minutes each day.

Once you've mastered the basics, move on to percents, decimals and fractions. For example, here is an example of expressing the same fraction three different ways:

As a fraction: 1/10
As a percentage: 10%
As a decimal: 0.10

Take a look at the chart called "A Fraction Is Part of a Whole" at the end of this chapter.

Then focus on:
- Time, distance, speed, space, volume.
- Interest rates: simple, compounded, amortized.
- Shopping and purchasing (how much of a product should a company buy at a time, for example).

You should be able to find simple practice problems in each of these areas online and in books.

ALGEBRA

Next up the math hierarchy comes algebra. Algebra is just a basic problem-solving process where letters represent different values, like distance, speed and time. It is key to learning higher math and science skills.

We use algebra regularly in everyday life to figure out things like: how much we're spending on groceries; how many miles our car is getting per gallon of gas; how much gas we can buy with the money in our pocket; how much each person owes when a group shares a meal together.

Facility with basic algebra is crucial for many career fields, including carpentry, engineering, market research, business and banking, and many more. Even fitness trainers use algebra to figure out the ratio of diet to exercise needed to lose weight and/or maintain it.

Many simple problems in algebra are available in books and on the Internet.

Here's a sample of a simple algebra problem:
Suppose Maria gathered 12 oranges and gave one third of them to John, her husband. To figure out how many John received, you would design the algebraic equation to describe this action as: X = 12 ÷ 3

Or, as a fraction: X = 12/3
This can also be written as: X = 12 x 1/3
The answer, then, would be: 4

GEOMETRY
Geometry is used to measure distance, direction (angles), area and volume.

It is a fundamental tool in many lines of work, including carpentry, engineering, interior design, surveying, navigation, mapping, even designing video games.

Here are a few critical bits of knowledge about geometry:

When dealing with all **right angles**:
1. To measure the area within a rectangle, multiply side A times side B.
2. The area of a square is one side squared (which, of course, is the same as side A times side B).
3. The volume of a cube is one side cubed, or length x width x height.
4. The volume of a three-dimensional rectangle, also called a "right rectangle prism," is the same — length x width x height, or the long side times the square of a short side.

When working with **triangles**, these facts are important to remember:
1. The three angles of a triangle always add up to 180 degrees.
2. In a "right triangle," one angle is always 90 degrees. The sum of the other two angles equals 90 degrees.
3. In a right triangle, side A squared plus side B squared equals the hypotenuse squared.

4. In an isosceles right triangle, the other two angles are equal, each 45 degrees.

5. If we know one angle and the length of one side of a right triangle, we can figure the other angle and sides.

When working with **circles**, remember these facts:

1. The circumference, the distance around a circle, equals Pi (3.1416) times its diameter (the distance across a circle). Pi is illustrated by the Greek letter π. C = π x d

2. The area within a circle is Pi times the square of its radius. The radius is half of the diameter. [equation π x r²]

3. The volume of a tube is the area of its cross section (i.e., the area of a circle) times its length.

4. The volume of a sphere is 4/3 times Pi times its radius cubed. V = (4/3) x Pi x r³.

Research online to find diagrams of each of the above. If you memorize these helpful mathematical facts and/or keep them handy, you'll find geometry much easier.

Sample exercise

Find the area of a circle with a 5-inch radius.

(See item 1 above — the formula is: πr², read as Pi times the square of the radius.)

(Answer: 3.14 X 25 square inches = 78.5 square inches)

TRIGONOMETRY

Trigonometry uses algebra and geometry to describe relationships between the sides and angles of triangles, especially right triangles. It's helpful to understand because every straight-sided shape, such as squares, rectangles and other polygons, can be divided into multiple triangles. Interestingly, it's also used when dealing with circles.

Trigonometry developed when Ancient Greek and Indian astronomers were trying to figure out distances between celestial bodies.

For practical purposes, it's used now in a variety of ways, for example in measuring the level of a sound wave or musical note. In engineering and architecture, trigonometry is used to calculate the slope of a roof and to create structurally safe buildings. Carpenters use trigonometry when making an angled cut on a board.

The six trigonometric functions are: sine (in diagrams often noted as "sin"), cosine (cos) and tangent (tan); and their opposites, secant (sec), cosecant (csc) and cotangent (cot).

In a right triangle, the sine of one of the other angles equals the length of the opposite side of that angle divided by the length of the hypotenuse. (In a right triangle, sine is always less than one, because the hypotenuse is the longest side of a triangle.)

Until used to solve problems, these may seem like meaningless, amorphous names. But when applied to real-life problems, they transition into valuable tools. For example, if you know the height and angle of a hill, you can figure the length of its slope and, with that, how much gravel and tar are needed to cover a new road being built on it.

Refer to the trigonometric angles chart at the end of this chapter and use, for example, 15 degrees and 45 degrees. Similar tables are available on the Internet. Cosine is similar, but is the side adjacent to the angle divided by the hypotenuse.

It may be difficult to gather adequate understanding of trig from instruction alone, but as you do a few simple problems, it becomes gradually clearer and clearer. Also, when you're doing trigonometry, if you're not provided with a diagram of the problem, draw one yourself.

Look for sample problems online, for example at www.onelinemathlearning.com.

See also charts called "Introduction to Trigonometric Functions" and "Sine, Cosine & Tangent" at end of this chapter.

PROBABILITY & STATISTICS PREVIEW

Statistics is the branch of mathematics that deals with the collection, organization, analysis, and interpretation of numerical data. It is especially useful in drawing general conclusions about a set of data from a sample of the data.

See Probability & Statistics Review chart (from Carson & Dellosa) at the end of this chapter.

CALCULUS

Still ascending the math hierarchy, we come to calculus. Every year about a million American students take calculus. But far fewer really understand what the subject is about or could tell you why they were learning it.

It's not their fault. There are so many techniques to master and so many new ideas to absorb that the overall framework is easy to miss.

Calculus is the mathematics of change. It describes everything from the spread of epidemics to the zigs and zags of a well-thrown curveball. The subject is gargantuan.

But within that bulk of information you'll find two ideas shining through: the "derivative" and the "integral."

Roughly speaking, the derivative tells you how fast something is changing. It helps you see how a pattern is likely to play out, whether it's a line or curve on a graph or a return on a financial investment. The derivative would be used to figure out, for example: marginal returns in economics; growth rates for investors or in demographics; the velocity, or rate of motion, of a body in relation to its changing position, in engineering, physics and astronomy; the slope of a hill or, on a graph, the rate of change of the steepness of the line or curve. (Steven Strogatz, N.Y. Times, April 11, 2010.)

The integral tells you how much something is accumulating, for example the area under a curve on a graph. Or, in practical terms, how much dirt would be needed to create a hill of a particular height. It can be used to create safer roads. It also is used in electronics to, for example, figure out the work or change in energy — how much heat will be given off — when two electric charges move toward each other or away from each other.

BOOKKEEPING AND ACCOUNTING

You may wish to start a business or get into management in a company where you're already working. Some familiarity with bookkeeping and accounting would be helpful. (If you've not used one before, find a basic calculator keyboard online.)

The basic reports in these realms are a Sales Journal and an Expense Journal and the Profit and Loss report that they generate. For a simple example, see charts at the end of this chapter. Many software programs are available to handle bookkeeping and accounting on the computer. Among the most popular are Quick Books and the templates available in Excel.

SUMMARY

Before taking on new math and science classes, you can develop an easy facility with math basics by doing easy exercises for just a few minutes each day.

In order to build math skills, first use flash cards for addition and multiplication until the answers come easily and automatically. (Skill in subtraction and division seems to accrue along with practice in adding and multiplication.)

Then, in each discipline, get good instruction (for example, by taking a community college course) along with doing practice math problems. You can find practice problems in books or on the Internet. Start with division, then long division, then squares, square roots and algebra.

Do several problems every day.

Work slowly from basic algebra to more advanced algebra, and then on through plane and solid geometry, trigonometry and calculus. Always relax and enjoy yourself before and during each session.

Classes in the various Computations skills are offered in most adult education programs and community colleges, as well as on the Internet.

Finally, two crucial understandings to carry away from this section:

1. Computations is a hierarchical skill, meaning you must establish ease with the basics in order to build your abilities with the next levels of math.

2. Math isn't learned from instruction alone. Understanding the concepts and gaining ease with solving problems come only from a combination of good teaching and practice — that is, doing a multiplicity of problems starting with simple ones and moving on to more and more complex ones.

Keep at it and one day you'll discover that math isn't difficult — it's fun!

On the following pages are the charts referred to in this chapter on Computations:

A Fraction Is Part of a Whole

$\frac{3}{4}$ of the circle is shaded. $\frac{1}{4}$ of the circle is not shaded.

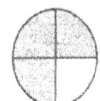

$\frac{3}{4}$ ← part shaded **numerator** part not shaded → $\frac{1}{4}$
    ← total parts **denominator** total parts →

On the first line, write the fraction for the part that is shaded. On the second line, write the fraction for the part that is not shaded.

1.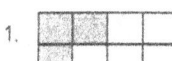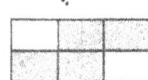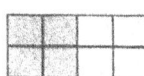

2.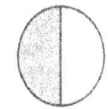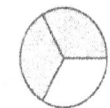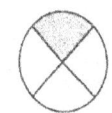

3.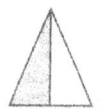

4.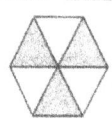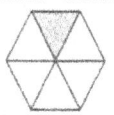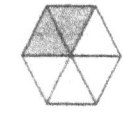

© Carson-Dellosa

INTRODUCTION TO TRIGONOMETRIC FUNCTIONS

Function	Abbreviation	Description
Sine	sin	opposite / hypotenuse
Cosine	cos	adjacent / hypotenuse
Tangent	tan (or tg)	opposite / adjacent
Cotangent	cot (or cotan or cotg or ctg or ctn)	adjacent / opposite
Secant	sec	hypotenuse / adjacent
Cosecant	csc (or cosec)	hypotenuse / opposite

For example,

Sine:

The sine of an angle is the ratio of the length of the opposite side (side of the triangle on which the angle *opens*.) to the length of the hypotenuse.

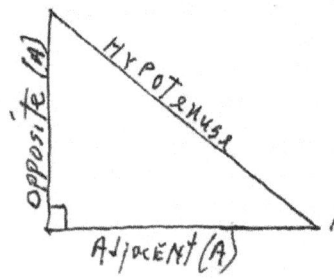

$$\text{Sin A} = \frac{\text{Opposite}}{\text{Hypotenuse}}$$

If Angle, A = 15°, sin A = .250
Then, if opposite side = 4, hyp = 16

If Angle, A = 45°, sin A = .700
Then if opposite side = 4, hyp =

4/hyp=.7, so .7 hyp = 4
4/.7 = 40/7 = 5 and 5/7

Sine, cosine, and tangent

The **sine** of an angle is the ratio of the length of the opposite side to the length of the hypotenuse. In our case

$$\sin A = \frac{\text{opposite}}{\text{hypotenuse}} = \frac{a}{h}$$

Note that this ratio does not depend on size of the particular right triangle chosen, since all such triangles are similar.

The **cosine** of an angle is the ratio of the length of the adjacent side to the length of the hypotenuse. In our case

$$\cos A = \frac{\text{adjacent}}{\text{hypotenuse}} = \frac{b}{h}$$

The **tangent** of an angle is the ratio of the length of the opposite side to the length of the adjacent side. In our case

$$\tan A = \frac{\text{opposite}}{\text{adjacent}} = \frac{a}{b}$$

The acronyms "SOHCAHTOA" ("Soak-a-toe", "Sock-a-toa", "Soak-a-toa", "So-kah-toa) and "OHSAHCOAT" are commonly used mnemonics to help remember these ratios.

[6 comp chart II]

Angle, A	opp/hyp	adj/hyp	opp/adj
5	0.089	0.995	0.089
10	0.175	0.989	0.177
15	0.250	0.960	0.250
20	0.336	0.938	0.358
25	0.436	0.911	0.471
30	0.500	0.866	0.570
35	0.550	0.821	0.644
40	0.644	0.762	0.844
45	0.700	0.700	1.000
50	0.762	0.644	1.200
55	0.821	0.550	1.446
60	0.866	0.500	1.730
65	0.911	0.436	2.120
70	0.931	0.345	2.700
75	0.960	0.250	3.800
80	0.989	0.175	5.200
85	0.995	0.089	11.176

Adding machine keyboard

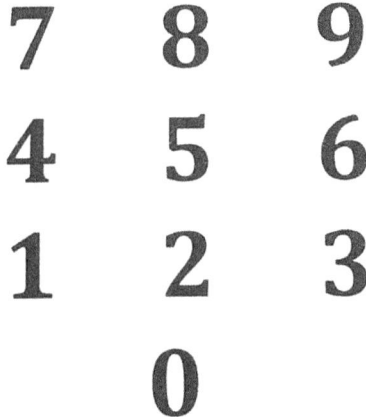

The 5 often has a bump on it to help locate the middle finger.
Use the middle finger for keys 2, 5 and 8
      The forefinger for keys 1, 4 and 7
    The fourth finger for keys 3, 6 and 9
        The thumb for key   0

Probability and Statistics Review

Probability is the chance or possibility that an event will happen.
- If the fraction that describes the probability is equal to 1, the event is certain.
- If the fraction is greater than another, the event is more likely.
- If the fraction is less than another, the event is less likely.
- If the fraction that describes the probability is 0, the event is impossible.

Find the probability. Write it as a fraction.

Penny has 11 pencils in her pencil box. Two pencils are orange, 3 pencils are blue, 5 pencils are yellow, and 1 pencil is green.

1. What is the probability that Penny will pull out an **orange** pencil?	2. What is the probability that Penny will pull out a **green** pencil?
3. What is the probability that Penny will pull out a **blue** pencil?	4. What is the probability that Penny will pull out a **black** pencil?
5. What is the probability that Penny will pull out a **yellow** pencil?	6. What color pencil is Penny **most likely** to pull out of her pencil box?

© Carson-Dellosa

[6 COMP CHART 14 EXPENSES JL]

EXPENSE JOURNAL
(simplified)

$ AMOUNT	ITEM
$15.00	PAPER TOWELS
$54.00	GAS
$85.00	SCREWS
$280.00	WOOD
TOTAL: $434.00	

[6 COMP CHART 15 P&L]

PROFIT AND LOSS STATEMENT
(simplified)

DATE	INCOME	EXPENSES	PROFIT/LOSS
FEB 12	$477.50	-$434.00	$43.50

SALES JOURNAL			
	($)		
CUSTOMER	SALES	CASH	RECEIVABLES
GEORGE	25.00	25.00	
CHEVRON	37.00		37.00
TOOL CO.	115.50		115.50
ARMSTRONG CO.	45.00	45.00	
HELENA, INC.	255.00		255.00
TOTALS:	477.50	70.00	407.50

(ACCOUNTING COURSE OUTLINE)

MONEY COMING IN
MONEY GOING OUT
MONEY OWED TO YOU
MONEY YOU OWE
THE BALANCE SHEET
THE INCOME STATEMENT
THE SALES JOURNAL
THE EXPENSE JOURNAL

REFERENCES & RESOURCES

Benjamin, Arthur T. *The Secrets of Mental Math*. Chantilly, VA: The Great Courses.

Benjamin, Arthur & Shermer, Michael. *Secrets of Mental Math*. New York, NY: Three Rivers Press, 2006.

Devaney, Robert L. *Mastering Differential Equations: The Visual Method*. Chantilly, VA: The Great Courses.

Griffin, Bitsy (Content Editor). *Skill Builders Math (Grade 4)*. Greensboro, NC: Carson- Dellosa, 2011.

Leaf, Brian. *Top 50 Skills for a Top Score ACT Math*. New York, NY: McGraw Hill, 2010.

Mitchell, Robert & Emory, Dolores. *Top 50 Math Skills for GED Success*. New York, NY: McGraw Hill, 2005.

Sellers, James A. *Mastering the Fundamentals of Mathematics*. Chantilly, VA: The Great Courses, 2012.

Skill Builders Math (Grades 3-5). Greensboro, NC: Carson-Dellosa, 2011.

Skill Builders Pre-Algebra (Grades 4-5). Greensboro, NC: Carson-Dellosa, 2011.

Skill Builders Geometry (Grades 6-8). Greensboro, NC: Carson-Dellosa, 2011.

Devlin, Keith. *Mathematical Thinking*. Stanford University Online course:

"Mathematical thinking is not the same as doing math. The goal of this course is to help course participants think the way that professional mathematicians think to solve real problems — problems that can arise from the everyday world, or from science, or from within mathematics itself. Anyone over the age of 17 can benefit from participating in this course, but it is primarily intended for high school seniors or first-year college students who are considering majoring in mathematics (or a mathematically dependent subject). The course will run for seven weeks and includes monitored discussion, group work, and an open-book final exam."

"Common sense in an uncommon degree is what the world calls wisdom."
— Samuel Taylor Coleridge

"Ideas are like rabbits. You get a couple and learn how to handle them, and pretty soon you have a dozen."
— John Steinbeck

"I believe that I am in hell, therefore I am there."
— Arthur Rimbaud

"I believe I am in heaven, therefore I am there."
— Skilligence®

CHAPTER EIGHT

SKILL 7: CONCEPT FORMATION

This chapter is, as you might guess, about forming concepts, about gathering ideas.
Probably the most helpful attitude for forming concepts is to keep an open mind, but as the skeptic maxim — attributed to both Mount Holyoke College professor Walter Kotschnig and British scientist Richard Dawkins — counsels, "Let's be open-minded, but not so open-minded that our brains drop out."

Our greatest power
One of the most important concepts to remember is the following definition of intelligence as: the ability to learn. More specifically, it is a very broad ability to learn — that is, new information and ideas, and

also new emotional responses, new attitudes, new behaviors and new behavior patterns.

Taking this further — and, yes, this is the founding principle of this book — intelligence is hugely improvable. It is a complex, hierarchical concept, and, when you understand it very well, it evolves from a process and ability into a dynamic skill.

This definition puts whole new dimensions on our understanding of the importance of intelligence, of how we think about it and how we act in regard to it.

If you think about it, intelligence truly should be our most treasured possession, the true source of our greatest power. And the ability to develop that intelligence is, indeed, our greatest privilege.

Exercise
What does that definition of intelligence mean to you?
(Write your answer in your notebook.)

According to the American Heritage Dictionary, Concept Formation is: the process of abstracting a quality or property of an object or event and then generalizing it to all appropriate objects or events. It is also a collection of percepts.

It's important to note that while the previous skill, Computations, primarily dealt with facts and absolutes, this chapter's skill, Concept Formation, deals with approximations, close or distant approximations of realities — that is, of what we think should be, of what we think may be, and of what we think is.

A PREVIEW

Although there are many pathways to forming concepts, this introduction to Concept Formation will focus on the following few:

- Guesses and estimates and checking them against reality
- Ausubel's top-down approach
- Gagné's bottom-up approach
- Keyes's six thinking skills
- Logic

Of those, most of our attention will be spent on the middle three: the approaches of David Ausubel, Robert Gagné, and Ken Keyes. And our primary focus will be on Keyes. The first and last, "Guesses-Estimates" and "Logic," may be the most important but are also somewhat self-explanatory. The middle three are less known and less taught now, and are equal contributors to an understanding of Concept Formation.

Edward De Bono's work also speaks importantly to Concept Formation, and while we will briefly touch on his "Six Thinking Hats" later in this chapter, we will reserve his other good ideas for the following two chapters, Problem Solving and Creativity.

First, a quick preview of the three on which we will focus:

1. Ausubel observed that we first learn about a subject with a vague, simplistic or approximate percept and then afterwards add important specifics.

2. Gagné noted that we best acquire useful concepts from the bottom up, acquiring important prerequisites first and then a broader understanding of the target concept.

3. Keyes offered us six thinking tools, which help us think and learn both accurately and adequately.

Here are some of the more important concepts we humans form as we mature:

· First, we must understand ourselves.

· Second, we must understand others and our relationships with them, especially our close relationships, and what is right and what is wrong in dealing with them.

· And thirdly, we must understand our community and our world, how they are now and how they have evolved, how they are evolving, and how and where we fit in them and in the world of work.

The more adequately and accurately we form these three concepts, the better we are able to direct and shape our lives.

Self-concept, briefly
In regard to ourselves, it seems helpful to get a good understanding of what we are and how we tend to see ourselves, along with some idea of the differences between those two, as well as the way we would like to be. We will delve into self-concept a little later in this chapter.

Relationships
In regard to our relationships, it is helpful to become aware of how we tend to view and relate to different people, and to practice what psychologists and philosophers suggest are good ways to relate, such as "active listening" and "I" messages," and to do it with tolerance, acceptance, understanding and love.

In regard to our relationship with our world, it's helpful to ask questions like: How long ago did our world start? When did animals and humans evolve? How are they similar and different? How large is our world? How many nations are there? Why are there wars? Can we abolish them? What are the ways to a world at peace?

Exercise

In order to strengthen the acquisition of your understandings of these associations, try keeping a three-part journal noting important facts and insights about yourself, your relationships and your world. You may find yourself reading more, and gathering interesting material to enter in this journal.

SELF-CONCEPT AND SELF-IMAGE:
THE POWER OF THE POSITIVE

A person's concept of herself or himself is a large facet of Concept Formation. It is worthy of at least several tomes all on its own, but for the purposes of this chapter, we will limit ourselves to a little exercise:

Think of a negative self-concept having to do with learning and intelligence and say it out loud. Then think of a correcting, positive self-concept and say it out loud.

Example: "I'm not good at math" versus "Math is easy and fun for me."

Recent research indicates that it takes four repetitions of a positive thought to temporarily replace a negative.

For most of us, negative thoughts about ourselves sometimes pop into our brains. Practicing positive responses instead can turn those positive thoughts into habits.

There are a couple of good books that can help you practice and reinforce your understanding of the power of positive responses:

"I'm OK — You're OK," by Thomas Harris, M.D., explores how we interact with others depending upon our self-concept. And "When the Past Is Present," by David Richo, helps us understand where negative self-messages come from.

In order to expand a bit further on our introduction to Concept Formation, take one of the quotes at the end of this chapter that you particularly like and read it out loud to yourself. Pay attention to how you feel afterwards.

A BRIEF CHRONICLE OF SOME
MAJOR POLITICAL & PHILOSOPHICAL CONCEPTS
Note that agricultural societies evolved about 12,000 years ago after some 200,000 years of hunter-gatherers

- **The Code of Hammurabi** (c. 1770 BCE, about 3,800 years ago): The first recorded code of law in human history, in what is now Iraq, provided laws and punishments that were applicable to citizens based on their social status and gender.
- **Moses** (c. 1300 BCE): The Ten Commandments, worship of and obedience to God and His teachings.
- **Solon** (c. 600 BCE): Solon's political reforms in Greece laid democracy's foundations.
- **The first democracy**: In Athens, Greece (c. 500 BCE).
- **Buddha** (c. 450 BCE): Acceptance of what is, meditation to Nirvana.

The Buddha's basic teachings are usually summarized using the device of the Four Noble Truths:
There is suffering.
There is the origination of suffering.
There is the cessation of suffering.
There is a path to the cessation of suffering.
The key to escape from this cycle is said to lie in the realization and acceptance that existence is characterized by suffering, impermanence and non-self.

- **Plato** (428-347 BCE): Discussed virtue, justice and reason. Advocated oligarchic government by the wisest philosophers.
- **Confucius** (145-c. 85 BCE): Respect for self, parents and state. Confucius regarded devotion to parents and older siblings as the most basic form of promoting the interests of others before one's own and taught that such altruism can be accomplished only by those who have learned self-discipline. Subjecting oneself to ritual does not, however, mean suppressing one's desires but, instead, learning how to balance and reconcile one's own desires with the needs of one's family and one's community.

- **Christ** (c. 0000): Love
- **Locke** (1632-1704): Tabula rasa. Humans are born with a mental blank slate. Sovereignty resides in the people. (A century later, his thoughts lead to democracy's first major reappearance after over 2,000 years.)
- **American Declaration of Independence**: American democratic government (1776).
- **A Menko Rose** (1925-) **prognostication**: All nation states will have democratic governments c. 2064; war is abolished, bombs are abolished, world is at peace, average IQ exceeds the old 125. (Understanding the past helps us understand the present and to predict and shape the future.)

GUESSING, ESTIMATING & CHECKING

Now that we have an overview of the great philosophical concepts of past and future that shape our present, let's get more formally into our personal Concept Forming.

Guessing or estimating is probably our most common method of Concept Forming. It doesn't make sense to take the time and effort to carefully investigate the complete, adequate and accurate description of every idea or object or activity we encounter as we go about our daily lives. So we acquire a percept or two of it and estimate the rest based on our existing knowledge. Then, in time, as we encounter the object or activity again and again, we compare our image, compiling additional information along the way, modifying our image gradually toward greater adequateness and accurateness. This casual method, I think, is wise sometimes. At many other times, however, when we need a more adequate and accurate concept, some rules are very worth learning.

≈≈≈≈≈

"Life," said Samuel Butler, the 19th century British author and satirist, *"is the art of drawing sufficient conclusions from insufficient premises."*

≈≈≈≈≈

KEYES'S SIX THINKING TOOLS

My favorite book, by far, on forming concepts is "How to Develop Your Thinking Ability," by Ken Keyes, Jr. He demonstrates habits of thinking that help us make what he calls "adequate verbal maps."

"Straight thinking," he says, "will tend to make your foresight as good as your hindsight."

Keyes emphasizes the use of "verbal maps" to describe reality, but adds that these verbal maps of reality must not only be accurate but also adequate.

To illustrate the difference, he tells the story a man who had an unhappy childhood and little formal education. This man's ambition to become an artist was bitterly opposed by his father. Although self-educated, he became the author of a book the sales of which in his country ranked next to the Bible. Obstacles did not discourage him. People would say, "Why, you can't do that!" But he hurdled one barrier after another. He placed a great deal of emphasis upon improving the health of young people, and he was known throughout the world as a dynamic speaker. His closest associate said of him that he "accomplishes great deeds out of the greatness of his heart, the passion of his will, and the goodness of his soul."

This is an accurate picture of Adolf Hitler…but not at all an adequate one. For he was also certainly one of the most evil men who has ever lived.

Keyes also urges the use of six tools for thinking:

1) The first of those thinking tools is: "**So Far as I Know.**"

As far as he knows, no human being knows all about anything. Can you think of anything about which your knowledge is complete? Can you answer every question about an automobile or a grain of sand, a pencil or an inch of sewing thread, a BB shot or a human being?

To repeat what Samuel Butler said: "Life is the art of drawing sufficient conclusions from insufficient premises." So, Keyes urged, when drawing conclusions, remind yourself that it is only "so far as I know."

Since our maps are not complete, we have no right to close our minds on any subject. Absolute certainty is a privilege of uneducated minds — and fanatics.

Except, that is, in math. For 2 of something plus 2 of the same thing is always 4 of the same thing.

2) Keyes' second thinking tool is: "**Up to a Point**."

This urges us to think in terms of degrees, and to recognize that most truths are true only up to a point. He said, "Look for the degree nature of things. And hunt for the point at which a little more may make more than a little difference."

An example is the familiar story of the nomad who added one straw at a time to his camel's back, assuming that the tiny added weight would not be noticed, until the poor camel's back broke.

The tool "Up to a Point" reminds us that things vary from none to all, and that we must stop, look, and listen to become familiar enough with the territory to make an adequate verbal map that has predictability.

Keyes's other four "tools" are just as pertinent and meaningful for forming concepts as these first two, and I urge you to do your own research to become familiar with them as well. They are:

"To Me,"
"The What Index,"
"The When Index" and
"The Where Index."

FROM THE BOTTOM UP
(From "Conditions of Learning," by Robert Gagné)
Pursuing the Concept Formation structure still further, it turns out that CF itself, like Computations, is often hierarchical in its structure.

An example of how success in learning requires building upon a hierarchical foundation is well shown in one study of learning a series of concepts:

Of those subjects who successfully attained one level in the series, 95 to 100 percent successfully attained the next higher level. When any level was missed, the probability of attaining the next level dropped markedly. For example, 71 succeeded at level 3A and 19 did not. All of the 71 who did succeed also succeeded at level 2A, the next higher level. Of the 19 who did not succeed, only 1 succeeded at level 2A. This pattern of predictability has been verified in a number of studies. (Gagné, 1965, p.153.)

Once the learner understands that complex Concept Formation is not a question of chance, but rather often a question of building prerequisite knowledge steps, he may learn to program this acquisition himself, in small chunks when necessary.

A reminder: Gagné's emphasis on prerequisite conditions applies in spades to Computations.

FROM THE TOP DOWN
(In "Psychology of Meaningful Verbal Learning," by David Ausubel)
If the learner learns further that while certain concepts, such as mathematical ones, seem to be best formed from the bottom up or from required parts to a whole (a là Gagné) and that other concepts such as learning theory may be best formed from the top down or from an amorphous whole to precise parts, (a la Ausubel), he will become a still more highly skilled concept-former.

For a current example of general to specific: When we explored intelligence, we first learned it is the "ability to learn." Then, in some greater detail, we learned that it is the ability to learn cognitions, emotions, behaviors and attitudes. Then, that it is hierarchical in nature. Then, that it has 10 major components. Then, that it operates with tools in an environment of modes and conditions, that it is first a process of learning, but also an ability to learn that can improve, and, finally, when you understand it very well, it becomes a skill that is best assumed to be infinitely improvable.

If, in addition, we learn that understanding a concept is often a matter of determining what it is and what it is not, and what it is similar to and different from. And further, that an optimum acquisition rate for complex concepts may call for deep relaxation while simpler ones will tolerate almost any level of tension and excitement, we will have taken significant additional steps in the acquisition of a powerful concept-forming skill.

LOGICAL REASONING

Deductive Reasoning: From a general premise to the specific.

For example: Men are hairy. Therefore, (I deduce) since I am a man, I am hairy.

Inductive Reasoning: From many specifics to the general

I note that most men have more body hair than most women. Therefore, I may conclude (induce) that, as far as I know, men are generally hairier than women.

In logic, a syllogism is a form of deductive reasoning consisting of a major premise, a minor premise, and a conclusion. A premise is an assumption that something is true. In logic, an argument requires a set of at least two declarative sentences, known as the premises," along with another declarative sentence known as the conclusion.

Aristotle held that any logical argument could be reduced to two premises and a conclusion. Premises are sometimes left unstated, in which case they are called "missing premises".

The proof of a conclusion depends on both the truth of the premises and the validity of the argument.

For example: All men are mortal. Socrates is a man. Therefore, Socrates is mortal.

This structure of two premises and one conclusion forms the basic argumentative structure. More complex arguments can use a series of rules to connect several premises to one conclusion, or to derive a number of conclusions from the original premises, which then act as premises for additional conclusions. An example of this is the use of the rules of inference found within symbolic logic.

DE BONO
De Bono's "Six Thinking Hats," a book and a tool for discussion, is intended to help facilitate group discussion, for example committees needing to reach agreement on decisions. But its messages are very useful for an individual's thinking process, for example attempting to acquire a complex and difficult concept.

The Six Thinking Hats
1. The White Hat (calls for information known or needed)
2. The Red Hat (signifies feelings, hunches and intuition)
3. The Black Hat (is judgment — the devil's advocate or why something may not work)
4. The Yellow Hat (symbolizes brightness and optimism)
5. The Green Hat (focuses on creativity — the possibilities, alternatives and new ideas)
6. The Blue Hat (used to manage the thinking process)

Exercise

Our concepts are often a matter of choice. We can choose, for example, to look at a half-full glass or at a half-empty glass. Our concepts of ourselves and the world around us affect the way we learn. See if you can work out
how your concepts affect your learning by answering the questions below:
(Write your answers in your notebook.)

- What concepts of your immediate and distant environment encourage learning?
- What concepts of your environment discourage learning?
- What concepts of yourself — what self-images — will encourage learning?
- What concepts of yourself will discourage learning?

Remind yourself regularly that self-talk, once thought to be a mark of craziness, is now recognized as a powerful force that can help you initiate and sustain the positive beliefs that lead you to satisfying successes.

RESEARCH
Finally, in order to form a concept more adequately and accurately, we must gather information from a variety of sources — that is, conduct your own research. It will be helpful to start your own library of reference works, or to bookmark online resources that you have found particularly helpful. This may include online dictionaries and other reference works, as well as websites and blogs devoted to your particular vocation or area of interest.

OVERVIEW RECAP
Concept Formation is simply generating an idea, an understanding. But some concepts are very complex and some have great power. They can enable us to do almost anything. And they can stop us from doing anything. They can even start a war, but also may some day help to bring peace.

Forming an accurate and adequate concept includes learning what it is and what it is not, what it is similar to and what it is different from. We form new concepts through deductive and inductive reasoning, through guessing, approximating and estimating.

And by following Keyes's counsel to make our concepts both accurate and adequate, using his six rules of thinking, we ensure that we make more reliable and predictive concepts. The many percepts that may be required to make a complex concept are available from many sources, including dictionaries, books, newspapers, journals, encyclopedia, search engines, and university courses — and also from brainstorming both individually and in a group.

The most important concepts from this chapter are:
1. Ken Keyes's Six Tools for Thinking
2. Guessing, estimating, approximating and checking

3. Gagnés two emphases: take the time and effort to learn prerequisites first (i.e., learning from the bottom up), and understand that many concepts have a hierarchical structure

4. Ausubel's emphasis on learning concepts from the top down or from the amorphous to the many details

5. Logical reasoning

6. The reminder that the first six component skills of intelligence, Relaxation through Computations, are prerequisite to the Concept Formation skill and that as they are developed, the Concept Formation skill improves

IN CONCLUSION:
CONCEPT FORMATION & WISDOM

The supreme importance of this chapter and of studying Concept Formation is supported by the common perception that a well-developed Concept Formation skill is wisdom.

At the very least, it surely may lead to wisdom.

Here are some wise quotes to make you think:

"It all depends on how we look at things, and not how they are in themselves."
—Carl Jung

"I believe in the human race. I believe in the warm heart. I believe in man's integrity. I believe in the goodness of a free society. And I believe that the society can remain good only as long as we are willing to fight for it — and to fight against whatever imperfections may exist."
—Jackie Robinson

"The fool doth think he is wise, but the wise man knows himself to be a fool."
—William Shakespeare

"Think left and think right and think low and think high oh, the thinks you can think up if only you try.
—Dr. Suess

"Those who dream by day are cognizant of many things that escape those who dream only at night."
—Edgar Allan Poe

"It is the mark of an educated mind to be able to entertain a thought without accepting it."
—Aristotle

"If you believe you can, you probably can. If you believe you won't, you most assuredly won't. Belief is the ignition switch that gets you off the launching pad."
—Denis Waitley

REFERENCES & RESOURCES

Allison, Jay & Gediman, Dan, Editors. *This I Believe: The personal philosophies of remarkable men and women.* New York, NY: Picador, 2006.

DeBono, Edward. *Six Thinking Hats.* New York, NY: Back Bay Books, 1985.

Durant, Will. *The Story of Philosophy.* New York, NY: Washington Square Press, 1952.

Grebstein, Lawrence C. *Toward Self-Understanding: Studies in personality and adjustment.* Glenview, Ill.: Scott Foresman, 1969.

Keyes, Kenneth S. Jr. *How to Develop Your Thinking Ability.* New York, NY: McGraw-Hill, 1950.

Morrow, Edward R. *This I Believe*, selections from the 1950s' radio series. This I Believe, Inc., 2010.

Pinker, Steven, *The Better Angels of Our Nature*, Viking. 2011.

"Positive Psychology: Harnessing the power of happiness, mindfulness, and inner strength," Harvard Medical School Special Health Report, 2013.

Richo, David. *When the Past Is Present: Healing the emotional wounds that sabotage our relationships.* Boston, Mass.: Shambhala, 2008.

Shermer, Michael, *The Moral Arc*, Holt, 2015.

CHAPTER NINE

SKILL 8: PROBLEM SOLVING

The ability to solve problems may be one of the truest measures of intelligence. We can form concepts all day long, but it is only the degree to which we use those concepts to solve our daily problems that makes our intelligence real and valuable.

In fact, the Problem Solving skill is often equated with intelligence itself. But it's not the same. Not quite.

Nonetheless, we do use problem-solving skills on an everyday basis. At home, we use them all the time — for example, when accomplishing chores or other jobs around the house and when dealing with relationships with our family members. At work, we use problem-solving skills to accomplish all sorts of tasks, as well as when we deal with co-worker, supervisor and subordinate staff relationships.

We also need problem-solving skills in order to plan for the acquisition of increments in our 10 component skills.

Interestingly, the Problem Solving skill may be more critical today than it was in the past. In the past, we might have often easily just followed in our parents' footsteps.

Today, we must cope with a volatile economy, with less stable work relationships (years ago, many workers would stay in one job their entire lives), and with ever-evolving technology regularly disrupting traditional work environments and a world in turbulent political transition.

These issues are all top priorities for us in understanding our place in this world. They also are all very difficult and complex issues.

For the returning veteran, making an often-times confusing transition to civilian status, possibly without strong family support, these difficult and complex issues may seem amplified. This chapter, along with the other skill chapters, is designed to help ease and surmount these challenges over a modest timeframe.

In this chapter, we will look at three different categories of Problem Solving: individual problem solving, which is our emphasis; group problem solving; and, lastly, couples problem solving.

We'll also learn some of the characteristics of skilled problem solvers. For example, among the most beneficial characteristics are: keeping your goal in mind at all times, being neither failure-phobic nor success-phobic, and being comfortable with trial-and-error learning. We'll learn more characteristics later in the chapter.

How Problem Solving contributes to intelligence
Our wellbeing and survival — as an individual, a family, a group, a nation or a species — depend directly on how well we solve problems and make decisions. In turn, how well we solve problems depends directly on our prior development of the seven prerequisite component-skills of intelligence: Relaxation, Attention, Motivation, Memory, Communications, Computations and Concept Formation.

Some parts of our life are determined by chance events substantially beyond our control. But, especially in a free society, most of us can determine a large proportion of our future ourselves. The values we arrive at, the goals we select, the skills we develop, the decisions we make, how we pursue them and how we meet the challenges fate presents to us along our way — the vigor, flexibility, patience and intelligence we put behind making and executing our decisions is our life.

According to English & English, authors of "The Comprehensive Dictionary of Psychological and Psychoanalytical Terms," 1958, Problem Solving is: "the process of selecting from a number of alternatives those that lead to a desired goal."

According to The American Heritage Dictionary, a problem is: a. A question to be considered, solved, or answered, or, b. A situation, matter, or person that presents perplexity or difficulty.

And, according to Wikipedia, Problem Solving consists of: "using generic or ad hoc methods, in an orderly manner, for finding solutions to specific problems."

All good definitions.

Many people actually equate Problem Solving with intelligence. But, again, it is not the same — not quite. It is close to intelligence, and it contributes mightily, but it is not equal.

Interestingly, Problem Solving may well be both the most important and most misunderstood skill. While we all like to think of ourselves as great problem-solvers, few of us likely really are.

Most of us may be good problem solvers in some areas while not so great in others. Which, incidentally, may be confusing to our inner self-concept.

As we've learned, Problem Solving is one of many prerequisites of intelligence. If any of the 10 skills, or prerequisites, including Problem Solving, is in short supply or missing, intelligence will be affected. The higher level of capability we build in each of the 10, the higher will be our intelligence.

Research indicates that chimps and even pigeons can improve their Problem Solving skills. I believe we humans haven't come close to the limit (if there is one) of how much the average person can develop his or her Problem Solving skills.

Research to date also indicates that when individuals who, despite some failures along the way, continue to successfully take on slightly more difficult challenges, they tend to improve their Problem Solving skills and their overall intelligence. Their self-confidence and self-image is likely to improve as well.

BUILDING YOUR PROBLEM SOLVING SKILLS

Problem Solving is the offspring of Concept Formation, and like other children, it is both dependent upon it and has a unique life and character all its own.

Problem Solving includes the Memory, Communications, Computations and Concept Formation processes we use to make decisions. Decision-making is one of the last steps in the Problem Solving process. It comes just before we begin to accomplish a task or create a product. Problem Solving is, therefore, often studied and written about under the heading of Decision Making.

There are a variety of ways to break down Problem Solving, but for our purposes we will use the following general modes: Impulsive, Intuitive, Trial-and-Error, Small-Step and Systematic.

1. **Impulsive** Problem Solving may be useful when we are pressed for time, the problem is simple and familiar, the consequences are insignificant, we are not too distracted by other disturbing problems, we can monitor the effects of our decision and we can modify it if it is not working well. Otherwise, a more considered response mode would seem advisable.

Impulsiveness is different from Intuitiveness. Impulsive Problem Solving is the use of the first solution we think of, without giving it or alternatives adequate consideration.

2. **Intuition** is the most misunderstood approach to Problem Solving. It seems to be used by both the very best problem solvers and the very worst.

Dictionaries define "intuition" as: an ability to understand or know something immediately based on feelings rather than with facts or conscious reasoning.

Those who use it well use it by drawing unconsciously from vast experience. Many poor problem solvers rely on Intuition without adequate experience. To solve problems they use their first impulsive responses. They assume they have acquired the expert's understanding without the expert's experience of what works and what doesn't. What they consider Intuitive is really more often Impulsive. Because their Intuition sometimes proves correct and even wise, they assume that their Intuition must always prove correct and wise. But it doesn't. Successful intuiting calls for extensive experience in a specific field or discipline.

3. **Trial-and-Error.** Both Impulsive and Intuitive Problem Solving are enhanced by Trial-and-Error Problem Solving. When we consider an Impulsive or Intuitive decision as the first of a series of trial decisions to consider and test, they too can be useful tools.

Some people find Trial-and-Error Problem Solving fun. They make it into a game. They appreciate it as a process of seeking a solution through a friendly maze of unknowns. The following four keys open the door to successful Trial-and-Error Problem Solving:

a. Accept that you do not know the solutions to many problems. Develop a relaxed open-mindedness.

b. Reduce excessive sensitivity to failures. Appreciate failures as learning experiences.

c. Expect to eliminate several alternatives on the way to an adequate solution.

d. Observe those who treat the Trial-and-Error process as an enjoyable self-development game, and imitate them.

In the T&E mode, we may try out a solution in imagery, or inquire how it worked for others, or try it out ourselves in real action. Depending upon the difficulty and importance of a problem, we may expect to find a solution after two, three, 20 or more trials. Thomas Edison is said to have tried a thousand solutions for a different problem. Writers and other artists may try a hundred ways to arrange a paragraph, a stage setting, a gesture, or a line of music until they find one that induces the cognitive and emotional response they seek.

Trial-and-Error is a vital supplement to other modes of Problem Solving, so that we can adapt our approach to assure adequate solutions.

4. The **Small-Step** approach is relied upon by many highly skilled problem-solvers. It consists of simply dividing a problem into smaller and smaller units until each can be easily solved. Then by solving each unit in turn, we solve the whole problem. We may also combine this

mode with the other three, using the Small-Step approach for part(s) of the problem.

This approach will come up again in the chapters on Creativity and Precision Learning.

5. **Systematic** approaches to solving problems are the most efficient. They are defined step-by-step procedures for specific kinds of problems, which have worked well for some people under some conditions. They are likely to lead us along the most direct path to a solution and to provide the highest probability of success. Systematic approaches have been designed to help us solve all kinds of problems: algebra and geometry problems; cooking, medical and legal problems; navigation, engineering, administration and financial problems; and philosophical, logical, psychological and personal problems too.

Most of the problems we face have been faced and solved by someone before us. For important problems, we are wise to take the time to learn about and use their successes and failures. If we do, we are more likely to succeed at whichever problem we face; and once we have established the habit of solving problems with Systematic approaches, we are likely to enjoy more successes with more challenges in the future.

In 1971, T.J. D'Zurilla and M.R. Goldfried found that highly skilled problem-solvers tend to follow similar procedures when they seek solutions to difficult problems.

See below for eight basic steps to follow when you're faced with a difficult problem.

When we want to solve a specific problem, such as how to: cook a spinach casserole, solve a marital conflict, find the third leg of a triangle, tune-up an auto engine or a piano, teach a child self-respect and responsibility, look for a job, overcome depression, feel and be energetic, budget, add beauty to one's life, work well and enjoy it, or learn anything difficult, we can rely on Trial-and-Error, which may be fun, or we can succeed far more quickly and surely by using a system that others have already tested and developed.

No two problems in life are precisely the same, so the best problem-solvers probably use all five of these general approaches. They use whichever is appropriate, sometimes separately, sometimes in combination.

EIGHT BASIC STEPS

For individual Problem Solving, this system of eight basic steps can be helpful:

1. **Identify and define the problem.** It is important to identify the core of the problem, or its precise goal, not the periphery.
2. **Gather Information.** Gather relevant information from experts. Consult books, articles and courses on Problem Solving for specific fields.
3. **Generate alternative steps to a solution.**
- **Relaxation.** If you're tense, you might grab at the first, not necessarily the best, solution.
- **Individual or group brainstorming** often helps to come up with a solution that you might not think of at first or on your own.
- **Seek out other ideas and solutions**, especially with good listeners, good reflectors and experts in a field.
4. **Evaluate the alternatives.** Judge probabilities and risk and reward. One technique to try is to rate each possible solution on a scale from 0 to 10.
5. **Select one and implement that solution.** Start with the first step.
6. **Assess the results.**
7. **If that first solution was not successful, try the next best idea.** Don't let failure define you. Desensitize yourself to failure, taking each as a learning experience, by reminding yourself of the Edison quote above. Try Chunking. Talk to yourself, motivate and re-motivate yourself.

If successful, generalize the solution to other similar problems.

7b. **Utilize other resources** to support additional attempts to solve the problem. Solutions include books, Internet, classes, puzzles, encyclopedia, library, experts, professionals, friends, family.

Or

8. **Accept that the problem may not be solvable right now.** You may not yet have the right tools to tackle this problem. You may have to come back to it at a later date when you have amassed those tools.

Exercise
Which problems are most important for you to solve at this time of your life? Do you think the above eight steps
will help?
(Write your answers in your notebook.)

CONTINUING TO IMPROVE
One critical set of problems facing you is how to continue to improve your intelligence when you complete this book or, if you're attending a class, when the class ends. This chapter will cover some ground, and we'll address it again during Precision Learning, but it is something that might be helpful for you to begin to think about now.

Devising a self-improvement program is like solving a problem, and without a plan, success is not likely to occur.

Exercise
What would help you schedule and implement the improvement of your overall learning ability, your intelligence? What problems do you foresee interfering?
(Write your answers in your notebook.)

Another important challenge we all need to solve: how to be happy. The Harvard Medical School offers a publication called "Positive

Psychology," which addresses that problem well. (See References and Resources.)

HOW TO

You may not learn to solve all of your difficult and important problems from a few pages in a book. You can, however, get a good introduction to the Problem Solving process with the following five exercises, one for each of the five modes of Problem Solving.

1) Impulsive Problem Solving is often propelled by impatience, anger, frustration and arrogance. Anger, frustration and arrogance are all normal and healthy responses in their places. But they are poor decision makers. When you put intensity into a decision, you tend to emotionally overvalue it; to defend it, justify it and hang on to it. When, instead, you relax deeply and think quickly of four alternative solutions for each impulsive decision you make, you begin to use the Impulsive mode wisely.

2) In the Intuitive mode, for a difficult problem, first state that problem simply, clearly and precisely. Write it down; read it; repeat it to yourself. Picture the problem — where you are now, the barriers; and the desired outcome. Picture them clearly and vividly. Then take time to relax deeply — every muscle in your body. Check especially muscles in and around your eyes, tongue and hand muscles. Deeply relaxed, serene and confident, wait patiently for the answers to come. As they come, don't judge them. Keep pen and paper handy; continue to relax deeply as you write the answers down, permitting more answers to come. After the fact, you may combine several answers into an adequate sequence of solutions for a complex problem.

3. To make Trial-and-Error skill development into a game, make a list of 10 problems. Each day, for just 10 minutes, take one of the 10 and see how many solutions you can think of. Put that number and the date on a card and graph it. Do the same each day and give yourself a reward whenever you exceed your previous record.

4. To build skill with the Small-Step mode, use a similar game plan. Again, make a list of 10 problems. Then for 10 minutes each day, see how many steps you can divide one of them into. Again, write the number on a card and graph it. Whenever you have exceeded your highest number of steps, give yourself a little reward.

5. For the Systematic mode, practice with this seven-step (A through G) introduction to family Problem Solving. Family problems may be the most important and difficult to solve. But success in solving family problems is also the most rewarding. Even apparently simple family problems may call for flexibility of approach and several trials. While this approach was designed for two members of a family, it may be adapted for more, and for other kinds of problems as well.

5A. Make a list of 10 simple family problems. Some may be made up. Rate them from zero (low) to 10 (high) for importance and difficulty. Several should be at a very low rating (zero or one) so that you can fail at them while you are still a beginner and it won't matter. The pain can be fierce when you fail at important family problems. So wait until you have developed expertise before you tackle the truly important ones.

5B. Relax deeply. Expert relaxers can often do it in a couple of minutes. For others, even with good instruction, it may take 10 to 30 minutes. The more important, difficult and complex the problem, the deeper you relax and the more thoroughly you monitor that you continue to relax. Practice talking and relaxing, talking and relaxing again, so that whenever you get aroused during discussion, you can relax once more easily and quickly.

5C. Each partner now takes a turn, or several, to define the problem. If you find it difficult to agree upon a definition (and this is not uncommon), be patient. The first problem may be to define the problem. If necessary, take the time to go through these seven steps to arrive at a mutually acceptable definition of the problem.

5D. While relaxed, each partner takes up to 10 minutes to express his or her feelings, perceptions and thoughts about the problem. While you express your feelings, perceptions and thoughts, your partner focuses on understanding them. He or she listens and accepts what you are saying as your point of view. From time to time, he or she also reflects, in slightly different words, what you are saying and what you seem to be feeling. Clarify whenever your partner has not picked you up reasonably well. Continue to take turns until each partner feels fully expressed and understood.

5E. Now, take turns suggesting solutions. Write them down. Reach for solutions, even unusual ones, that may please both partners. Each partner encourages the other's suggestions and rigorously avoids any evaluations of the suggestions in this step.

5F. Pick a solution. Judge which solution will provide the greatest long-term comfort and benefit for both partners. If helpful, each partner may rate the suggested solution from zero to 10. The solution with the highest combined rating is a prime candidate for the first trial. Look patiently until a solution acceptable to both is found.

While you practice steps C though F, a voice recorder can give you feedback about how well you share and listen, how relaxed you stay and how supportive you manage to be for each other.

5G. Try it. Carry out the decision and monitor the effects. Be ready to go through the Problem Solving process again when either partner becomes dissatisfied.

If you practice this process on simple problems for one half-hour a week, you will develop expertise rapidly. At least in the beginning, the problem should be so simple they really don't need this powerful a tool, and so unimportant that you can try frequently and fail fearlessly. Then when you need the skill for a difficult problem, as Anaïs Nin said of the writing process, much of it will be honed and automated, in reliable working order ready for use.

PRACTICE, PRACTICE, PRACTICE

Now, it is time for us to actually practice Problem Solving. Let's start with this little algebra problem: As we start, take a moment to observe your body. Are you relaxed?

Here's the problem:

Drake took a total of eight quizzes over the course of the first four weeks. After attending five weeks of school this quarter, How many quizzes will Drake have taken in total?

Assume the relationship is directly proportional.

First, make the appropriate equation, using "X" for the unknown. What does "X" represent? ($X = 8 \times 5/4$)

This exercise is to remind you of one good way to build Problem Solving skills: do loads and loads of algebra problems. Good ones may be found in *Pre-Algebra* and *Algebra* from the Skill Builders series, Carson-Dellosa Publishing.)

GROUP PROBLEM SOLVING

Edward de Bono, in *Six Thinking Hats*, teaches thinking and decision making as a greatly improvable skill. "The main difficulty of thinking is confusion," he writes. Better thinking involves thinking in only one mode at a time, rather than attempting all thinking modes at once. He labels six different modes of thinking as:

- White Hat: gathering information about facts and figures.
- Red Hat: for expression of opinions, feelings and emotions.
- Black Hat: for expression of caution and critiques.
- Yellow Hat: for the positive, hopeful view.
- Green Hat: for fertility — generating new and different ideas.
- Blue Hat: the organizing and implementing hat.

His book is aimed at groups, but it is useful for individuals as well. In the next chapter on Creativity, we'll use his *Lateral Thinking* book. It also applies to both individual and group Problem Solving.

It is crucial during group Problem Solving that members of the group listen to each other and reflect often on what is being said for clarification.

Refer also to the list of publications and resources at the end of this chapter. Problem-Solving training is available at many schools and on the Internet.

COUPLES PROBLEM SOLVING

Couples Problem Solving is a unique challenge. The intimacy and frequently intense need for affection and high regard from the other, combined with the normal but conflicting need for both dominance and attachment, along with other innate expectations and the often great importance to a whole family of the relationship, make this territory both fragile and complex and at the same time critical to happiness and the welfare of all concerned.

For this reason, for many couples, special measures need to be available. The help of a skilled, non-judgmental marriage therapist or group may be worth considering.

Use of the three skills, Relaxation, Communications — especially the use of active listening and "I messages" — and Problem Solving, are especially helpful. Used in a gentle, loving and disciplined way, together, they raise the probability of successful Problem Solving greatly.

(Review the Relaxation and Communications chapters for exercises in Relaxation and "I messages" and "Reflecting.")

Begin by scheduling short discussion sessions about easy, non-threatening subjects. Give each other gentle feedback about your impression of the other's use of the Relaxation, Communications and Problem Solving skills. After satisfactory experiences with short sessions and the easiest of subjects, try slightly longer sessions and slightly more difficult issues.

Important note: *One person cannot solve couple problems.*

Characteristics that support Problem Solving by couples:

- Intention to (and creation of habit patterns that) support each other

- Understanding and acceptance of one's natural tendencies toward competitiveness, dominance and submissiveness as well as conflict, and a willingness to overcome them
- Good communications skills: listening, sending and sharing
- Ability and willingness to see from the partner's point of view
- Gentleness
- Flexibility and a sense of humor
- Facility with, and appreciation of, Problem Solving processes
- Ability to hear about and make each other's needs and wishes known

The use of your Relaxation, Attention, Motivation and Memory skills, along with facility with Trial-and-Error, will be helpful in developing better levels of each of these characteristics.

Here's one suggestion for a program for couples:
1. Agree to listen to each other positively and supportively
2. Agree to speak with "I messages" and without blame
3. Take short, one to five-minute turns speaking, while the other listens and reflects. Limit talks to 30 minutes, less in the beginning.
4. Each prepares ahead of time what to say
5. Each identifies what is good about the other and the relationship
6. In several separate sessions, each identifies changes desired.
7. When speaking or listening, pull away when you feel yourself tightening or getting negative or blaming.
8. Each responds to one change request with either a commitment to make the change or, if necessary, what would make it easier to make that change, or that no change seems possible.
9. Practice tolerance and acceptance of the other's feelings and also of yourself, acknowledging that mistakes will be made along the way.

PHOBIAS & ANXIETIES

De Bono cautions us that confusion blurs our thinking and Problem Solving. He advises us to use only one of his six "thinking hats" at a time in order to get clarity. And that is good advice. But another fierce and common inhibitor of thinking and Problem Solving is high anxiety and the corresponding phobic response. Particularly common is the fear of failure, and perhaps equally so, for some of us, the fear of success and also the related fear of mathematics. All three may occur together.

It is beyond the ability of this book to cope with this problem. But I can offer a couple of suggestions. Mainly, become aware and mindful of such feelings. Journal frequently about them. Relax deeply when you do. Let the Flame of Attention gradually soften and dissolve these feelings. Practice replacing them with positive feelings.

Chunking also helps. Divide the problem into tiny elements and attend only to the next small challenge.

Eye Movement Desensitization and Deep Muscle Relaxation (EMDR) with small-step desensitization described in the Relaxation chapter are also effective. If the problem is intense and entrenched, professional help should be considered from a behavioral therapist skilled in these processes. Our principal message in this section is: Don't let phobia or anxiety keep you from being a great learner. Even if you have been hampered by them for years, you can now be freed of these nasty limitations.

Word puzzles
Do Cryptograms and Jumbles to improve your skills
with Problem Solving.
(For cryptograms, some hints: The words "the," "that," "it is," "it's," "people," "I'm," "you," "your," and "you're" are common letter patterns to look for.)

Rearranging letter patterns seems to exercise the brain's neuron complexes in a way very similar to what is required to rearrange your attitudes and habits to better solve
everyday problems.

COLLECTING IDEAS
Another great tool for Problem Solving is brainstorming.
   Whether conducted by a couple or in an individual's journal or by a group, a few rules raise the probability that a brainstorming session will be productive for problem solving:
   • Anyone who has an idea can share it.
   • No one will comment either positively or negatively on any of the ideas during the brainstorm.
   • No one will ask questions or discuss any of the ideas until after the brainstorm.
   • When all the ideas are out and listed, go over anything that needs clarification.

Characteristics of a skilled problem solver
   • Keeps goal in mind at all times
   • Neither failure-phobic nor success-phobic
   • Comfortable with trial-and-error learning
   • Patient, flexible, persuasive
   • Communicates with clarity
   • An accomplisher and a chunker
   • Resilient
   • Confident (of finding a solution)
   • Good listener, respectful of other viewpoints
   • Searches for prerequisites, similar challenges, relevant information, advice, a mentor
   • A reader (reading about prerequisites, similar challenges, etc. as above)
   • Energetic (do your best and your best will be growing better)
   • A decision-maker
   • Possesses self-understanding and self-acceptance
   • Lateral and vertical thinker
   (For any characteristic not adequately possessed, it helps to identify and develop each, one little bit at a time.)

IN A NUTSHELL:
How do you build Problem Solving skill?

The answer is, a little at a time. Like any other skill, you build its prerequisites, the other nine components of intelligence, along with your patience and your resilience and your relaxed energy and perhaps above all, your ability to use failures as stepping-stones.

At the same time — and this is crucial — you practice taking on, at first, a variety of many, very easy problems, and then, following successes and growing confidence, very gradually, more difficult and complex and important ones.

In fact, to repeat, research has shown that people who do this alone — that is, successfully take on gradually greater challenges — do raise their intelligence. This chapter's suggestions will accelerate that progress.

≈≈≈≈≈

Remember the "Tree"

When addressing the problem of how to make the most of each of these chapters, we suggest using the "Tree." Draw a tree for each chapter, using the main branches and twigs to identify the sections and their sub-ideas that are most important to you. Review each tree from time to time to integrate that chapter into your understanding of the whole of intelligence. This chunking process allows you to focus your learning energies on what is most important to you.

≈≈≈≈≈

REFERENCES & RESOURCES

Alberti, Robert & Emmons, Michael. *Your Perfect Right: Assertiveness and equality in your life and relationships.* Atascadero, CA: Impact Publishers, 2008.

Bosco, David. *Rough Justice: The International Criminal Court in a World of Power Politics.* New York, NY: Oxford University Press, 2014.

Bolton, Robert, Ph.D. *People Skills: How to assert yourself, listen to others, and resolve conflicts.* Upper Saddle River, NJ: Prentice Hall, 1979.

Brockman, John. *Thinking: The New Science of Decision-Making, Problem-Solving, and Prediction.* New York, NY: Harper Perennial, 2013.

Christine Junge, Editor. *Positive Psychology – Harnessing the power of happiness, mindfulness, and inner strength.* Harvard Medical School Special Health Report, 2014.

DeBono, Edward. *Lateral Thinking.* New York, NY: Harper & Row, 1979. Keyes, Ken, Jr. *The Hundredth Monkey.* Coos Bay, OR: Vision Books, 1987.

TerKeurst, Lysa. *Unglued: Making Wise Choices in the Midst of Raw Emotions.* Grand Rapids, MI: Zondervan, 2012.

"Have confidence that if you have done a little thing well, you can do a bigger thing well too."
– David Storey

"Accomplishment is the most important thing."
– Arnold Hutschnecker

"Do your best and your best will be growing better."
– Emma Hart Willard

"The most creative thing you can do is to energize and create yourself gradually closer to your favorite image of yourself."
—Menko Rose III

CHAPTER TEN

SKILL 9: CREATIVITY

How do we define Creativity? Most of us likely would agree that Creativity is, quite simply, the ability to accomplish something that is to some degree original as well as useful or beautiful.

Robert Franken expands on this simple definition in his academic work "Human Motivation," defining it as "the tendency to generate or recognize ideas, alternatives or possibilities that may be useful in solving problems, communicating with others, and entertaining ourselves and others."

The website "Creativity at Work" also has a useful description: "the act of turning new and imaginative ideas into reality. [It] is characterized by the ability to perceive the world in new ways, to find hidden patterns, to make connections between seemingly unrelated phenomena, and to generate solutions." It then adds: "Creativity involves two processes: thinking, then producing."

An interesting elaboration follows that description — it says, "If you have ideas and don't act on them, you are imaginative but not creative."

Therefore, one must actually produce, or accomplish something — a goal, a task, a project, a piece of art — in order to be creative.

Critically key to Creativity, then, is, indeed, accomplishment.

Dictionaries and discussions of Creativity emphasize originality. But, just as Thomas Edison, one of the most prodigiously creative individuals of all time, once noted about genius — that it is "one percent inspiration, 99 percent perspiration" — so it goes for creativity.

Truly, creativity is 99 percent accomplishment. The other one percent is originality.

The dictionary tells us that to "accomplish" is to complete something. But when we look with greater discrimination at what is involved, we find there is more to accomplishment than that. It is the ability to start, do and complete something.

Putting it all together, then, for us Creativity is: the ability to start, do and complete something new or different that is also to some degree useful or beautiful. The more competence we acquire at beginning, doing and completing things, the more creative we are able to become.

BREAKING IT DOWN
For our purposes, Creativity can be broken into three essential elements: vision, learning and accomplishment.

Here are some basic steps to help you progress on your path to improving your Creativity via these elements:

Vision
The first step is to gradually shape an idea, a vision, of what you intend to create. Then adjust that idea, clarifying it, honing it more

and more precisely. Then — and this is super-important — keep that goal, your vision, in mind at all times.

Learning

There are several ways of approaching the learning component, including: inheritance, imitation, instruction, trial and error, prerequisite skills development and persistent improvement.

Here's a brief breakdown of how to use these seven avenues to help boost your creativity:

Inheritance: Identify and take full advantage of your inherited advantages. For example, you might have an innate facility for drawing, for art, or for more easily understanding numbers and math. Figure out how to use your advantages to achieve your goals.

Imitation: Imitate several of those you admire who are talented and expert in your chosen field.

Instruction: Get the best instruction and mentoring you can find, afford and cope with.

Trial & Error: Practice accepting and learning from failures, turning them into future successes.

Prerequisite Skills: Develop to high levels your prerequisite skills, that is, Relaxation through Precision Learning. Facility with these prerequisites will make your progress easier, faster and surer.

Persistent Improvement: Keep working at improving.

Accomplishment

As we've learned, Creativity is all about accomplishment — that is, getting good at accomplishing things, first small tasks, then bigger ones.

It's very like the well-known Nike brand tagline: "Just do it!"

Just accomplish things. Create tasks — goals — for yourself, and accomplish them.

Remember, Creativity is 99 percent accomplishment. The more you accomplish tasks and goals, the better you will get at accomplishing future goals and the more creative you likely will become.

Creativity is also the ability and courage to imagine and to make mistakes — to not be afraid of failing — part of traveling and accomplishing in the unknown.

Of course, what is considered "creative" is also subjective. Just as beauty, for example, is very much "in the eye of the beholder," what seems like junk to me may seem very creative to someone else. And vice versa.

Here are four basic steps to help you develop facility and skill in accomplishment:

1. Practice, practice, practice! Accomplish, accomplish, accomplish!

Work on the simplest, easiest tasks at first. Then, very gradually, work on slightly more complex and difficult tasks. Continue to practice and strengthen your accomplishment habits, facility and skills with very simple and easy tasks.

If you're hard-pressed for tasks to practice with, why not work on building the more basic components of intelligence — the Communications and Computations skills, for examples?

2. Learn to enjoy accomplishing things, by focusing on and reinforcing your progress. For example, decide what would be a treat for you — whether it's a small piece of chocolate or a short walk around the block — and use that as your reinforcement when you make progress.

3. Allow yourself to dream just a little, while keeping your goal in mind at all times. Let the power of that vision pull you forward.

4. Despite setbacks, continue to improve.

You've probably noticed that these are the same principals and procedures to build each of the individual skills of Skilligence, as well as to build overall intelligence. So, keep working on building the more basic skill-components of intelligence — it'll help your progress in every aspect of every skill.

≈≈≈≈≈

A few of my favorite quotes about accomplishment and Creativity:

"Accomplishment is the most important thing."
—Arnold Hutschnecker, psychiatrist and author of "The Will to Live"

"Failing to prepare is preparing to fail."
—Benjamin Franklin, leading author, inventor, scientist, statesman and one of the founding fathers of the United States

"The will to succeed is important, but what is more important is the will to prepare."
—Bobby Knight, one of the most successful college basketball coaches of all time

"Keep your goal in mind at all times."
—Arnold Hutschnecker

≈≈≈≈≈

MORE ON ACCOMPLISHMENT

That's a pretty big, bold claim — "accomplishment is the most important thing."

Let's take a closer look at what we mean by "accomplishment," because it can be a broad term.

A good, general definition for our purposes is: the successful achievement or completion of a task, a job, a project — perhaps a piece of art or writing.

So, getting good at "accomplishment," then, means getting good at completing tasks, jobs, projects.

Many times accomplishing a project means breaking that project down into multiple pieces, multiple tasks — also known as, yes, you guessed it, "chunking" — and then accomplishing each of those tasks, or chunks.

Exercise
(Record your answers in your notebook.)
Is accomplishment really the most important thing?
Is it really more important than love?
More important than friendship?
More important than creativity?

Now, ask yourself this: Can any of these even exist without accomplishment? Can they exist at a high level without high-level accomplishment?

BREAKING CREATIVITY DOWN FURTHER
Now that you understand how Creativity and accomplishment are interlinked, let's delve a little deeper.

Here are seven critical components of Creativity; each may be cultivated and improved:

1. Knowledge of and familiarity with the field in which your goal exists For example, writers read, singers listen, painters copy and observe, etc.

2. A fair level of general and specific prerequisite skills
No matter what your goal is — swimming or writing, cooking or playing the violin, baseball or business management — build the basics. It's the same advice winning Olympians like Mark Spitz and Michael Phelps give to aspiring swimmers: Build. The. Basics.

With the Skilligence® Framework, we use all of the "basic" skills, from Relaxation through Problem Solving, in every accomplishment. And when a task requires us to learn something new and difficult, the 10th skill, Precision Learning, is also helpful. The more proficient we become at all nine of these foundational skills, the better accomplishers we become and the more creative potential we gain.

3. A modest level of vision and innovativeness

(Check out Edward de Bono's book "Lateral Thinking"; see some highlights of de Bono's "Lateral Thinking" later in this chapter.

4. Ease with trial-and-error, imitation and instruction

Become comfortable failing. That may seem counter-intuitive, but it's a truly vital facet of successful people's personalities. As an example, think about skiers — they must be comfortable falling before they can become good at skiing.

Most successful people have failed multiple times on the pathway to reach their goals. But their key characteristic is that they're good at shaking off the failure and continuing their quest for success.

The legendary silent film star Charlie Chaplin tried a scene 100 different ways before he felt it was right. The famous Argentine author Jorge Luis Borges rewrote his articles over 100 times before permitting them to be published. Ernest Hemingway rewrote the ending for "A Farewell to Arms" 39 times. August Rodin continued to sketch and sculpt hands, feet, heads, torsos, individuals and the whole group of his Burghers of Calais until he felt his statue adequately projected both the simplicity and the nobility of the sacrifice these men had made.

Business consultant Tom Peters, author of "A Passion for Excellence," advises his clients: "Do it, fix it, try it."

In the trial-and error mode, we keep our goal in mind and accomplish as well as we can, knowing we cannot do anything perfectly. As Peters suggests, as we accomplish we continuously seek ways to improve our performance.

Learn to accept your failures and use them to improve at your goal. Failure is a vital part of the accomplishment process. Successes tell us what works. Failures tell us what doesn't.

Learn also to welcome praise and criticism about what you are doing well and not so well. Remind yourself that, with the feedback, you are getting better and better.

For important accomplishments, obtain competent instruction and coaching. Observe and imitate skilled individuals. Learn with others who are developing similar skills. Set long-term goals and work toward them in small steps.

And finally, to build and maintain motivation, keep your goal in mind and chart and celebrate your progress.

5. At least modest self-confidence and self-worth

If you have trouble in this area, review the Motivation chapter and try self-talk.

Remember, you can use positive self-talk as a powerful tool to boost your self-confidence and quash negative emotions that tend to depress your feelings of self-worth.

Recognize also that you will have mixed feelings, also referred to as "ambivalences," about your self and your ability to become successful. Learn to replace those negative self-images and expectations — of being a failure, of being unloved — with positive ones.

6. Expectations graded gently, from modest to high

This is where "chunking" becomes helpful. In fact, dividing accomplishments into small steps may be the most valuable sub-skill.

As with any skill, it is best to practice it regularly with a variety of simple challenges. Each day, divide a simple task into steps. For example, writing a letter: find the envelope, the paper, the address, the stamp; write the address, the salutation; think what you want to say (in general and then in specific); write the first word or two, the first phrase, and so on.

Once you have automated the habit of dividing a simple task into small steps, begin to practice dividing more complex and difficult tasks into segments. The smaller and more familiar the segments, and the smaller the steps of each segment, the more accomplishment leverage you generate.

An Arab proverb can help get us started: "The longest journey begins with just one step." This is reinforced by Henry Ford's quote, "Nothing is particularly hard when you divide it into small jobs."

Even the simplest task has a number of steps; and common accomplishments, such as preparing a meal, may have hundreds. If we were always aware of all those steps, we would confuse and slow ourselves down.

Once we have automated the steps of a task, we can look at the task as a single, integrated accomplishment. All we have to do is get started and our automatic pilot will take us through to completion.

But when a task is not familiar, many of us still try to accomplish it in one fell swoop. We try to force the new accomplishment through any old automated sequence of habits. It doesn't work. We push harder. We tense more. We tie ourselves into knots, frustration and failure.

In order to succeed, we need to retreat, take time to relax, attend freshly with relaxed eyes to the task, divide it into a new series of small steps, and accomplish those small steps one at a time. Start each, do each and complete each — the essence of accomplishment.

7. High-level accomplishment habits and skills

Above all, Creativity requires competence and high-level accomplishment skills. The development of this competence can be both simple and complex. We can learn to do something better in small steps, to acquire degrees of competence. In small steps we can identify, learn, overlearn and automate succeeding levels of knowledge, understanding and skill.

To assure the acquisition of important and difficult competencies, we may apply all of the principles of learning described in this book.

PERSISTENCE AND PRACTICE

So, then, Creativity is mostly accomplishment. Small steps, organization and preparation are among the keys to accomplishment. Vision and inspiration are important too, but, according to Jensen, persistence and determination are vital along with practice, practice, practice.

You may have heard a version of the following famous and oft-told classic joke:

A young woman carrying a violin was walking east in a rush along the south side of broad, busy 57th Street in midtown Manhattan when she encountered a tall, distinguished-looking gentleman headed in the other direction. He had long white hair and wore a black fedora and a long black overcoat. She asked him, "Excuse me, kind sir, could you please tell me, how do I get to Carnegie Hall?"

He looked at her most kindly, paused just a bit, and said, "My dear, my dear, of course. Practice. Practice. Practice."

≈≈≈≈≈

Practice. Practice. Practice.
Another, more personal story to
illustrate the benefit of preparation and practice.

I left Wall Street after I had been fired from my last three jobs. Somehow, I irritated the senior partner at the last firm. I still don't know how or why.

Badly depressed, I went for counseling to Arnold Hutschnecker, M.D. He was the author of "The Will to Live." He counseled many prominent entertainers of the day as well as President Richard Nixon. When I told him I had decided to become a professional folk singer (when inebriated, I would play the guitar and sing with my friend Artie Bach at our parties), among other things, Hutschnecker advised me as follows:

"A poor amateur musician practices one hour a day. A fair amateur practices two hours a day. A good amateur practices three hours a day. A poor professional practices four hours a day. A good professional practices five hours a day. A great professional practices six hours a day."

When he told me that, I practiced nine hours a day — three hours in the morning, then a two-hour break, then three hours in the afternoon, another two-hour break, and finally, three more hours in the evening. I became a modestly talented professional folk singer-guitar player in about six months.

I performed mostly at public schools. In those six months, I went from one good performance and nine poor ones to the reverse, nine good performances and one poor one. This required in the beginning that I survive the nine out of 10 failures. For me, then, it was worthwhile. Maybe I was trying to impress my new bride or my new children, three still to come. I seemed to have no choice.

Had I stayed with it for longer than three years, would I have become a lot better and a lot more successful? I'll never know. I didn't know how to relax then, so I may not have.

≈≈≈≈≈

EDWARD DE BONO'S LATERAL THINKING

Edward de Bono is considered by many as the leading voice on creativity and innovation through his work on self-organizing systems, specifically the neural networks of the brain.

He originated the term "Lateral Thinking," which most people think of as "Creativity" and which refers to the process of solving problems through "an indirect and creative approach." It literally refers to coming at a problem from the side — essentially, like the common saying "thinking outside the box."

As a contrast, "Vertical Thinking" is approaching a problem using conventional, linear, logical processes.

Here are a few key points about Lateral Thinking; some are direct quotes from de Bono's book of the same name:

• Lateral thinking is concerned with the generation of new ideas. New ideas are the stuff of change and progress in every field from science to art, from politics to personal happiness.

• "Lateral thinking is the process of using information to bring about creativity and insight restructuring." The rearrangement of information into another pattern is insight restructuring. The purpose of the rearrangement is to find a better and more effective pattern for your purpose.

- Vertical thinking (normal deductive and inductive reasoning) is concerned with proving or developing concept patterns. Lateral thinking is concerned with restructuring such patterns (insight) and provoking new ones (creativity). Lateral and vertical thinking are complementary. Skill in both vertical and lateral thinking is necessary for Creativity.

- Lateral thinking uses information provocatively. It breaks down old patterns in order to liberate information and stimulates new pattern formation by juxtaposing unlikely information.

- More and more, creativity is coming to be valued as the essential ingredient in change and in progress.

- "Lateral thinking can be learned, practiced and used. It is possible to acquire skill in it just as it is possible to acquire skill in mathematics."

- In using de Bono's book "Lateral Thinking," it is important to remember that practice is far more important than understanding of the process. (As we've come to understand, this applies to Skilligence® skills as well.)

- The purpose of thinking is to collect information and to make the best possible use of it.

- De Bono created "Po" as the principal tool for Lateral Thinking. He calls it the "laxative of language." The first function of Po is creating new arrangements of information. The second function of Po is to challenge old arrangements of information.

- Lateral thinking is directed towards bringing about changes in ideas through deliberate insight restructuring rather than (traditionally) through conflict and debate.

- "In order to develop skill in Lateral Thinking, one must practice and go on practicing, and that is why there has been such emphasis in this book on practice sessions."

De Bono's book "Lateral Thinking" is well worth a read and contains exercises to help improve lateral thinking.

Do!
Creativity is often a matter of rearranging part of reality. I find Jumble puzzles helpful to loosen the "muscles" in my brain. Cryptograms, also, are a great exercise to strengthen your creative muscles.

You can find Jumble puzzles and Cryptograms in newspapers or online. When you start doing these puzzles, don't worry too much about getting them all right. Just keep doing them easily. Don't give them too much time. Accept that you will get some right and fail at others. Gradually, more and more quickly, you will get more and more of them correct.

Do! If you want to become and remain a high-level accomplisher and achiever: Do! Do! Do!

Don't get sucked in by the couch or TV. Exercise physically, mentally and emotionally to keep the blood flowing and the body toned.

In order to get my own "do" going, I still do puzzles and little exercises every morning.

HIGHER LEVELS

Now, how does one get to the higher levels of Creativity? Well, turns out, there are many ways.

First, it's a good idea to make it a habit to check your basic skill levels as you take on different creativity and accomplishment challenges.

Exercise

1) How do the following prerequisite skills influence your Creativity and Accomplishment?

Relaxation, Attention, Motivation, Memory, Communications, Computations
Concept Formation
Our Concept of the goal and challenge
Our Self-Concept
Our Concept of our community, country and our world
Problem Solving (and one of its major components:
Trial and Error)

2) And, on a scale of 1 to 10, where do you see your skill level in each of these prerequisites?

(Write your answers in your notebook.)

Visualize

Now, sit back and make yourself as comfortable as you can. Tense and relax a few muscles and then let your whole body become deeply relaxed.

Then, visualize or dream of what you would like to be doing one year or five years or 10 years from now.

What would you like to use your developing understanding of Skilligence® for? Just let the images come. Don't select any until one or more stay with you.

As the visions appear, enjoy them for a few moments and then open your eyes and write down your fantasy in your notebook.

Now, divide the distance from where you are now to that goal into five to 10 steps. Don't try to make it perfect on your first stab at it. Approximations, even guesses, are quite good enough for now.

In the next chapter, you'll find tips to help you clarify the steps and add a reinforcement idea for each step.

It may be both pleasant and wise to go through this relaxation, visualization and chunking process periodically.

Core Steps

As previously noted, it is difficult to teach Creativity in general. It is easier to teach singing or guitar playing or writing or sketching or public speaking.

But here are some core ways of developing competence and creative skills:

• Do many easy, simple, familiar tasks first. Acquire the success habit, the easy, confident, accomplishing habit, along with the ability to identify and handle the little details and problems that often make a big difference. Remember that simpler, more familiar tasks require less relaxation skill and attention. So, continue practicing and entrenching the success habit with simple, relatively familiar tasks. And then, relax and re-relax frequently with the new and more difficult ones.

• Identify and desensitize yourself to anxiety blocks and the many (necessary) failures along the way.

• Zero in on your natural tendencies, the positive ones.

• Get the best instruction and/or mentor(s).

• Then, keep your goal in mind at all times! And Chunk! And Practice!

• And, over time, imitate highly skilled individuals — several of them. Eventually integrate what you learn from them into your own unique style.

Also, get your tasks readied the night before or the hour before. Get your working tools out and organized.

Another thing I find helpful is to remind myself regularly of this quote by Bobby Knight, the famous college basketball coach: "The will to succeed is important, but what's more important is the will to prepare."

You also might benefit from studying the famous UCLA basketball coach John Wooden's "Pyramid of Success." It is easily found by doing a Google search on "John Wooden Pyramid."

Some characteristics of creative people
They tend to:
• develop facility with the Trial-and-Error Mode, taking each "failure" as a learning opportunity and experience;
• achieve successes with simple challenges, then gradually take on slightly more difficult, complex, longer, less familiar tasks;
• continue to practice the basics with simple, easy, fun tasks, thereby entrenching the easy accomplishment and success habit;
• rehearse regularly and frequently, clearly imagining themselves successful and enjoying it;
• be interested in, but generally less concerned about, the opinions of others.
• And, perhaps most importantly, they are persistent!

FINAL THOUGHTS ON
CREATIVITY & ACCOMPLISHMENT

Creativity-Accomplishment is at the peak of the learning hierarchy. All of the eight previously discussed learning skills exist solely to feed and nurture this ninth skill. Even at their highest levels, the more basic skills can acquire their meaningfulness only when expressed through Accomplishment.

In your process and practice of developing your Creativity and accomplishment skills, remember to be patient. Keep in mind that it generally takes 10 years to hone a difficult art or skill to a dependably high level. Keep in mind also that a small skill improvement may have a large positive effect.

Remember to enjoy the process of accomplishing — if you do you likely will become a most creative, constructive and contributing individual.

Also remember that achieving accomplishment skill in almost anything will support achieving accomplishment skills in others.

Although it's true that great accomplishment skills will not guarantee high creativity, you can be sure that 100 people with great accomplishment skills will achieve many, many times more, and at a far higher creativity level, than what 100 people with low accomplishment skills may achieve.

So, first become a great accomplisher, and then go ahead, let yourself dream a little about that challenge you've been putting on the back burner.

More of my favorite quotes

"A poem begins in delight and ends in wisdom."
—Robert Frost

"Act well at the moment, and you have performed a good action for all eternity."
—Johann Kaspar Lavater

"Don't look for your dreams to come true; Look to become true to your dreams."
—Michael Beckwith

*"It matters not what goal you seek —
its secret here reposes.
You've got to dig from week to week,
to get results or Roses."*
—Edgar Albert Guest

"Have confidence that if you have done a little thing well, you can do a bigger thing well too."
—David Storey

"I have not failed. I've just found ten thousand ways that won't work."
—Thomas Alva Edison

"I am only one, but I am one. I cannot do everything, but I can do something. And I will not let what I cannot do interfere with what I can do."
— Edward Everett Hale

"When love and skill work together, expect a masterpiece."
—John Ruskin

"Creativity is allowing yourself to make mistakes. Art is knowing which ones to keep."
—Scott Adams

"Dreams come a size too big so that we can grow into them."
—Josie Bisset

"By failing to prepare, you are preparing to fail."
—Benjamin Franklin

"Those who dream by day are cognizant of many things that escape those who dream only at night."
—Edgar Allan Poe

"One does not discover new lands without consenting to lose sight of the shore for a very long time."
—Andre Gide

"The world we live in is the world we create."
—Dr. Thomas R. Bennett

"Nothing is as real as a dream ... because the dream is within you, no one can take it away."
—Tom Clancy

REFERENCES & RESOURCES

Buzan, Tony. *Use Both Sides of Your Brain.* New York: NY: Plume, 1991.

Colvin, Geoff. *Talent Is Overrated.* New York, NY: Portfolio, 2008.

Covey, Stephen R. *The 7 Habits of Highly Effective People: Powerful Lessons in Personal Change.* New York, NY: Free Press, 1989.

Coyle, Daniel. *The Talent Code.* New York, NY: Bantam, 2009.

Csikszentmihalyi, Mihaly. *Creativity, Flow and the Psychology of Discovery and Invention.* New York, NY: Harper Perennial, 1996.

De Bono, Edward. *Creativity Workout, 62 Exercises to Unlock Your Most Creative Ideas.* Berkeley, CA: Ulysses Press, 2008.

De Bono, Edward. *Lateral Thinking.* New York, NY: Harper Perennial, 1990.

De Bono, Edward. *Serious Creativity.* New York, NY: Harper Business, 1992.

Doidge, Norman, M.D. *The Brain That Changes Itself.* New York, NY: Penguin, 2007.

Franken, Robert E. *Human Motivation*, 3rd Ed. Boston, MA: Brooks-Cole Publishing Company, 1994.

Hanson, Rick. *Hardwiring Happiness: The New Brain Science of Contentment, Calm, and Confidence.* New York, NY: Harmony, 2013.

Johnson, Steven. *Where Good Ideas Come From.* New York, NY: Riverhead, 2010.

Katz, Nikki. *The Everything Cryptograms Book.* New York, NY: F&W Publications, 2005.

Koestler, Arthur. *The Act of Creation.* New York, NY: Penguin, 1990.

Carlson, Richard. *Don't Sweat the Small Stuff and It's All Small Stuff: Simple Ways To Keep The Little Things From Taking Over Your Life.* New York, NY: Hachette Books, 1996.

Michalko, Michael. *Thinkpak: A Brainstorming Card Deck.* Berkeley, CA: Ten Speed Press, 2006.

Root-Bernstein, Robert S. Root-Bernstein, Michele M. *Sparks of Genius: The Thirteen Thinking Tools of the World's Most Creative People.* Boston, MA: Mariner Books, 2001.

Siegel, Daniel J. *Mindsight: The New Science of Personal Transformation.* New York, NY: Bantam, 2010.

"Wisdom does not show itself so much in precept as in life — in firmness of mind and mastery of appetite."
— Seneca

"Luck is infatuated with the efficient."
— Proverb
(And Precision Learning means efficient learning.)

CHAPTER ELEVEN

SKILL 10: PRECISION LEARNING

OK, this is it — Precision Learning is the key.
Precision Learning is the key that enables an adult to use the Skilligence® system to systematically and successfully build her or his intelligence.

A Precision Learner is a Precision Teacher who teaches herself or himself. In fact, most books on improving learning skills note that a good learner is one who is first a good teacher and then uses his or her teaching skills to teach him- or herself.

In fact, education researchers have long known that when young student learners take part in both programming and choosing reinforcers, learning is amplified.

Lovitt and Curtiss found that when the choice of reinforcers was turned over in part to the student, and when, within limits, the choice of which studies to undertake at which time was made by the student, response rates increased. In both instances, learning was faster than when choices were made by the instructor alone.

And, Mager and Clark found that when students programmed their own learning from materials offered, learning tended to be more efficient.

Precision Learning is a powerful learning tool. Each of us can turn the power of this tool to improving the nine more basic components of intelligence — Relaxation and Attention through Concept Formation, Problem Solving and Creativity. It is the key we use to convert these abilities into skills.

To carry the metaphor a bit further, each person's key is going to be a bit different. We each must shape this key for ourselves. Others can give us information and instruction, but from the information and instruction, each of us must forge our own key and adapt it for our own needs.

OVERVIEW
Precision Learning is a set of procedures highly skilled teachers use to assure that their students learn things that are very difficult for them. The procedures were initially developed at the University of Washington; they were then further honed there and at the universities of Kansas and Oregon.

Interestingly, Precision Learning's power is in proportion to its precision. Most of the time, we don't need it at full power. We only use it at the level of precision we need for a particular task. We can focus it on a minute learning task, such as increasing our ability to memorize from five digits to six digits or increasing our ability to attend to a book from 10 seconds to 12 seconds.

We can also focus its power onto a global learning task, such as increasing our intelligence.

The six steps, or procedures, are simple, and they are of equal importance. While we may apply just one and still succeed at a simple learning task, we may need to apply all six to succeed at a difficult one. And we will need to use all six with increased precision and combine them with relaxation, as well, to assure success with our most complex and difficult learning challenges.

The six steps are:
1. **Goal Identification**. Identify a precise learning goal and then describe it in detail in writing.
2. **Baseline Determination**. Determine current levels of relevant knowledge and skills — that is, what levels of the goal's prerequisite behaviors, knowledge and skills are already possessed by the learner.
3. **Small-Step Programming**. Identify and create a program of small, readily accomplished learning steps from baseline to goal.
4. **Reinforcement**. Schedule appropriate reinforcers for each step of learning progress.
5. **Continuous Measurement**. Continuously measure progress from step to step in responses per minute whenever feasible. (An example would be words per minute for someone improving reading speed and comprehension, or writing for someone aiming to become a professional writer, or number of minutes for someone sharpening her/his ability to focus.)
6. **Program Modification**. Each of the first five processes are reviewed and modified whenever learning progress is not adequate.

The simplicity of each of these six learning steps may be deceiving. Each is fairly simple on its own, but when combined together their joint power is awesome. Even alone and at modest levels, Precision Learning skills can work small wonders.

When faced with a difficult learning or accomplishment challenge, these six simple Precision Learning processes can help you raise the probability of success by orders of magnitude.

Here's a little closer look at how to approach each of them. Later in the chapter we'll delve even deeper.

1. For **Goal Identification**, clearly identify and precisely describe your learning goal. There must be no ambiguity about it. To hit the bull's eye, a rifle must be aimed directly at its center. Nothing leads more quickly to vague learning effort than a vague learning goal.

The more precisely we identify our goal, the more powerfully it pulls us towards it.

2. **Baseline Determination** depends on Step 1, Goal Identification. We determine the level of skills and knowledge we have on each of the continuums that lead to the goal. In turn, the next three steps — Small Step Programming, Continuous Measurement and Reinforcers — also depend on an accurate determination of baseline.

The baseline is where we start. It is the foundation. When baselines are inaccurate and shaky, all subsequent steps will be as well, and therefore proportionately less effective. When they are too high, failure rather than learning will result; and when too low, the program may be tiresome and boring. When the baseline is accurate and precise, we have a strong foundation for our learning program, and progress is more likely to be secure and rapid.

3. **Small-Step Programming,** from the baseline to the goal, is the core of Precision Learning. Its power is illustrated by the story of the husky young man who repeatedly tried to scale a 30-foot-high smooth wall and repeatedly failed, with only bruises and a twisted ankle to show for his effort.

Finally, on the suggestion of a friend who was a precision learner, he stepped back and relaxed, and then built a series of 59 six-inch-high platforms, one on top of another, each a bit narrower than the next. It was a bit slow, but the probability of his success had gone from zero to 100 percent. Slowly but surely he walked up the steps he created to the top of the wall.

Learning programs work the same way. When we divide them into small enough steps, difficult ones become easy, and impossible ones often become possible.

4. **Reinforcers** are given following a response. When conditions are consistent, or at least similar, reinforcers increase the probability and frequency of the response. With them, our reasoning processes arouse support from our emotional processes. They help us weaken bad habits and strengthen good ones.

Pay is a reinforcer. So is praise. Few of us work well without both. Children and adults who do not receive reinforcers for learning do not learn.

The power of a reinforcer changes. What is reinforcing for one person at one time is not necessarily reinforcing at another time or for another person. When we are thirsty, a sip of water is reinforcing. Right after a long drink, it will not be.

When we are hungry for attention, even a scolding may be reinforcing. When we are hungry for love, it will not be.

In the beginning of a program, frequent, regular reinforcers are helpful. As the learning progresses and internal reinforcers begin to take over, fewer and more intermittent external reinforcers have a more powerful and longer lasting effect on us.

5. **Continuous Measurement** and feedback about progress from one step to the next is another powerful learning tool. It alone may multiply the learning rate.

To accomplish it, we identify and count responses (number of vocabulary words memorized per minute, for example), then record them on a sheet and on a graph. As the graph line goes up or down from baseline, we get visual feedback about our progress, just as though we were observing ourselves climb each of the 59 steps in the example for Step 3. We don't have to wait three weeks or two months for a test. We get immediate feedback about our rate of progress.

Continuous Measurement tools tell us whether new learning behaviors are taking us toward or away from our goal. If, following a new reinforcer or new arrangement of learning steps, learning slows, we know to adjust it. If learning accelerates, we know to stay with the new trial. A rise in the shape of the graph, reflecting an acceleration of learning, often generates such a powerful motivation that external reinforcers become less important.

6. **Program Modification** is a common need; it is to be expected. Initial program designs regularly require modification. One of the advantages of continuous measurement tools is that they permit us to experiment with a program change and receive immediate feedback about how well it is working.

This set of Precision Learning tools can be focused onto a micro-learning program, such as increasing reading speed from 100 words per minute to 150 or onto an intermediate-size program, such as losing 15 pounds of weight, or onto a macro-program, such as increasing intelligence from 110 IQ to 120 IQ.

The latter would have 10 sub-programs, one for each of the 10 components of intelligence. In turn, each of them would have several sub-programs. A program for Precision Learning, for example, might have six sub-programs, one to hone each of the six tools we have just discussed.

Exercise

Write down one important goal in the space below. Identify the goal; establish the baseline; program steps from baseline to goal, and schedule reinforcements.

ACTION PLANS
Another critical Precision Learning tool
Action plans involve setting goals, creating hierarchies, and prioritizing; and then making decisions about which skill and at what level to start.

An action plan is something you want to do and decide to do. It is achievable and action-specific. And it has a confidence of success level of 7 or more on a scale of 0 to 10.

An action plan answers each of these questions:
- Specifically, what will you do?
- How much will you do?
- When will you do it?
- How often?

Remember to identify your goal, estimate your baseline, estimate and program at least several steps, schedule reinforcements and measure progress.

Review your goal from the exercise above and see how it fits into the action plan above.

SELF-DISCIPLINE

A critical component of Precision Learning is self-discipline.

Here is an excerpt from an op-ed in the Monterey, California Herald newspaper from 1997 that captures my beliefs on the need for teaching responsibility and self-discipline:

"I think parents are missing the boat if they think that all they have to do is be sure their kids are happy, smart and creative. I believe that responsibility and self-discipline are every bit as important. …

"I think that a truly successful person would have intelligence, creativity, confidence, and responsibility. The sense of responsibility would be based on self-discipline and concern for others. These are the things we need to teach young children, whose attitudes and values are largely formed before age 8.

"As children become school-agers and teens, they also need to learn some other important things:

• To sort, prioritize and evaluate information in order to make wise choices.

• To have realistic expectations instead of instant gratification.

• To be able to relax without being constantly entertained.

• To feel they belong as part of the family, a circle of friends, and as part of the community and the world."

– Evelyn Petersen, educator, Monterey County Herald, November 30, 1997

If your parents forgot to help you acquire self-discipline, this is an excellent time to remind yourself of its great value and to initiate a program to develop it.

IMPORTANCE AND RELATIONSHIPS

Precision Learning is the key to the city of our golden dreams. It is what we most need to assure our success and enjoyment when we embark on a program to approach our intelligence and each of its components as a skill.

Learning Precision Learning is a little difficult at first, but after a while, it can become relaxed and automatic.

Learning it is also like learning to drive in that it gives us freedom. But the freedom is more magnificent. It is the freedom to learn.

The first nine components of intelligence are prerequisites of Precision Learning. It, in turn, is a prerequisite of each of them becoming a skill.

Precision Learning evolved from, and is a combination of, the other nine components of intelligence. Its first purpose is to focus back upon them, to permit us to improve them with a very high probability of success, to engage greater power as we convert each of them into a skill.

Another important function of Precision Learning is to help us make learning into a game. Games have rules. The six steps described earlier (and elaborated on below) are the rules with which we play this learning game. We compete with ourselves, with our own previous records and baselines. We celebrate and reward ourselves — perhaps with our friends or a group who share our purposes — whenever we do well.

HOW TO

Precision Learning methods simplify otherwise difficult learning tasks and help to make the learning into a game. Like any game, it takes a little time to learn the rules. But once we do, we play better and enjoy the game more.

To help turn your learning into a game, below are introductory instructions for each of the six steps or procedures: identifying your goal, determining your baseline, programming small learning steps, measuring progress, scheduling reinforcement and modifying the learning program.

We can progress rapidly and enjoy learning to use these tools more when we make it into a game. For example, give yourself a prize for a simple precise goal, an accurate baseline, an easily accomplished series of learning steps, an effective reinforcer, clear feedback about progress, and for a productive program change.

Goal Identification: If we aim generally and casually at a target, we might hit it, but it's more likely we will not. On the other hand, if we take careful aim and attend precisely to the bull's eye or the head of a nail, our chances of hitting it will increase remarkably.

So that we can find it and take aim precisely at the very center of a learning goal, we must verbalize it with pinpoint precision.

"To increase intelligence" is an acceptable goal, but for Precision Learning it is really just an initial approximation. "To increase Memory skills" is a move in the right direction. "To increase the rate of Spanish words memorized and recalled correctly in a 10-minute session" is almost there.

Identifying the set of 1,000 cards with, say, a Spanish-English vocabulary word on each will provide us with the additional precision we need.

Baseline Determination: It's easy to determine a baseline when the goal is stated as precisely as above. It is important to determine the baseline before learning begins so that progress will be evident immediately as it occurs. This clearly observed progress toward a valued goal provides the most powerful reinforcement. It is just like a strong wind pushing a sailboat toward its chosen port.

In order to determine the baseline for memorizing Spanish vocabulary words, we memorize a different set of words for 10 minutes on Monday, Wednesday and Friday prior to beginning the actual program. We divide the total number of words memorized during these three sessions by 30 (three sessions of 10 minutes each) to give the average number of words memorized per minute. That is our baseline. Any improvement above that level is progress.

Small-Step Programming: There are many ways to program small learning steps. The Spanish vocabulary words may first be learned in groups of five. Once we learn each group, we can combine two of them to make a pack of 10 for review, then two of these to make twenty, and so on to groups of 40, 80, 100, 200, 400, 800, and finally, 1,000. At each level there may be two steps. First we learn them in a consistent order and then in mixed order (shuffled each time).

Continuous Measurement and Feedback: We need a data collection sheet or card and a graph for each learning program. A lined 3x5 card can serve as our data collection sheet each week, and on the next page is our graph. Using log graph paper is even better because it can represent almost unlimited improvement.

The card shows the number of words we memorized in each of three 10-minute sessions on Monday, Thursday and Friday. The graph shows the baseline and the average rate per minute for each day. It leaves room for substantial improvement. This simple counting, recording and feedback skill is the most powerful learning tool in existence.

Reinforcement: Reinforcers help too, particularly in the beginning. They should be small. They should not overwhelm the accomplishment or obscure the intrinsic or natural environmental reinforcers (i.e., feeling good about each success). They serve as a bridge, not a replacement, for the intrinsic and natural reinforcers.

They are a means of communicating approval to the autonomic nervous system and to the emotional system. Therefore reinforcers, at least in the beginning, should be administered immediately following the desired behavior. This permits the autonomic system to associate the good feeling from the reinforcer with the cognitively desired behavior. It helps the cognitive domain overcome conflicts and bad habits that have been programmed into the autonomic nervous system.

Both small, concrete reinforcers and tokens for larger rewards seem to be effective for most people. To make a reinforcer schedule, collect a list of desirable rewards. Select a few of them for each learning program with the understanding that this is the only way you can obtain these reinforcers during this period. For sips of water or a peanut, the abstinence time between reinforcers may be no longer than an hour, while for a new music album, it may be six months.

We can provide ourselves with reinforcers for both the number of words memorized and for increases in the rate of memorizing. For example, we might decide to give a point for every word memorized in the beginning and then, as our skill continues to develop, for every five and then 10 words. We may also give a point for every tenth of a word-per-minute increase in rate.

Program Modification: To develop the Program Modification skill, it's best to try different things: early morning sessions, different reinforcers, a different schedule of reinforcers, a more precisely defined goal, and, of course, dividing learning steps into smaller steps. Our continuous feedback system tells us immediately what works well and what doesn't.

Our programs need not be perfect. Fair ones are often reasonably productive and can be refined as we go. We can use them as models and can refer to a specific skill chapter and suggested readings for additional program ideas.

Precision Learning is, in one sense, the simplest, most natural and primitive of all skills. We just aim carefully and precisely at where we are going and begin to move in that direction in small steps, checking regularly to see that we are continuing in our chosen direction. As Tom Peters told us in the last chapter, "Do it. Fix it. Try it."

Remember, these brief instructions will get you started. Don't forget to do your own research — look up additional resources on each of the six procedures.

PRECISION LEARNING IN A NUTSHELL
Precision Learning takes place when we use Precision Teaching skills to teach ourselves. Its six steps are: Goal Identification, Baseline Determination, Small-Step Programming, Continuous Measurement and Feedback about Progress, Reinforcement and Program Modification. Any one of these may accelerate the learning rate. All together they form a powerhouse set of learning tools.

The power of Precision Learning combined with the concept that intelligence is a skill permits an almost infinite, self-directed enlargement of the human potential.

General skill-building processes
- In order to assure progress, specific time must be set aside for skill building.
- The baseline and goal must be identified and recorded.
- A means to measure and record progress must be set up and kept handy.
- A schedule must be set up to reinforce progress.

Suggestions on implementation
Once the goal is chosen, keep it in the front of your mind. In order to maintain your momentum, schedule variety within the program.

Resist non-programmed distractions. For example, work on building one skill for three weeks, then shift to another.

Schedule regular breaks with refreshing activities. Experiment with what works best for you. I do a Sudoku or a Jumble puzzle.

You are the teacher, responsible for the whole intelligence-building program. It will work well as soon as you design and implement this program. Taking classes in the skills will also help a lot.

Also check out the sample Action Plans in the next chapter.

Exercise
(Write your answers in your notebook.)
What sort of short breaks (brain-clearers) would work for you?
What will you plan to do for longer-term breaks?
What are the advantages of building a skill solo?
What are the advantages of building a skill with a partner or a group?
How does humor facilitate serious skill building?

❖ ❖ ❖

Notes on reinforcement
(For more on reinforcements, see the Motivation chapter.)

• Self-reinforcement, using these guidelines, may be the most powerful tool you will have for strengthening your motivation, for increasing your intelligence and for developing a reliable and sustainable learning power.

• Make an initial quick list of what works for you for reinforcement.

• As your own Precision Teacher, decide which to use as program reinforcements. Remember to use them only for that purpose.

• Research has shown that it is best to reinforce every success in the beginning, and then to taper reinforcements for every other success, and then every third success, until succeeding becomes second nature and self-reinforcing.

• Remember that reinforcements should be small. They should inspire a strong desire for more. If they are too large, they will smother the desire for more. When you schedule reinforcements for yourself, keep this in mind. If you don't quickly have an urge for more, you've over-stimulated (not reinforced) yourself.

Exercise

Ask a friend to share an important life goal. Help your friend identify the goal, establish the baseline, program steps from baseline to goal, and schedule reinforcements.

REFERENCES AND RESOURCES

Butler-Bowdon, Tom. *50 Self-Help Classics*. Boston, MA: Nicholas Brealey Publishing, 2003.

Coyle, Daniel. *The Little Book of Talent: 52 Tips for Improving Your Skills*. New York, NY: Bantam, 2012.

Doidge, Norman, M.D. *The Brain that Changes Itself: Stories of Personal Triumph from the Frontiers of Brain Science*. New York, NY: Penguin, 2007.

Hall, Stephen S. *Wisdom: From Philosophy to Neuroscience*. New York, NY: Knopf, 2010.

Meacham, Merle L. & Wiesen, Allen E. *Changing Classroom Behavior: A Manual for Precision Teaching*. Scranton, PA: International Textbook Co., 1969.

Meier, David. *The Accelerated Learning Handbook*. New York, NY: McGraw Hill, 2000.

Patterson, Gerald R. and Gullion, Elizabeth M. *Living With Children: New Methods for Parents and Teachers*. Champaign, IL: Research Press, 1968. (Very useful for parenting yourself.)

"If we treat people as if they were what they ought to be, we help them become what they are capable of becoming."
—Goethe
(Will you treat yourself as you ought to be?)

CHAPTER TWELVE

IMPLEMENTATION

In this last chapter, you will take center stage.

This Implementation chapter will help you get started — it will help you use Precision Learning to make an initial Action Plan for developing one of the 10 component skills of intelligence. After that, you can use what you learn here to create Action Plans for the rest of the skills.

Also in this chapter, we will review important elements of Skilligence.

First, before we get into the Action Plans, here are a few reminders and suggestions for best practices as you navigate your way to success in achieving your learning goals:

1. Remember to work initially with very simple, easy challenges. As you succeed, try slightly increasing levels of difficulty and complexity. Your intelligence will build and build and build.

2. If possible, work with a learning buddy. *The Power of Two*, by Brian and Gerri Monaghan, discusses the enhanced power individuals derive from working together. For some, the same principle will apply to intelligence building.

3. Neuropsychological research has shown a correlation between humor and intelligence. Humor — enjoying fun and feeling happiness — increases the release of dopamine in the brain, which has been shown to aid in learning, specifically in creativity, problem solving and memory.

Exercise
Where does humor fit in with intelligence for you?
(*Write your answer in your notebook.*)

4. Intelligence was once thought to be over 90% inherited. Then, during most of the last century, it was thought to be an ability affected to a limited degree by the early environment. Now we know that it is very improvable, but we don't know just how much. So it is best considered to be infinitely improvable in adulthood by developing the 10 component skills of intelligence. Improvements in each of the 10 improve intelligence.

5. Now, to refresh your memory of the Skilligence Framework:
The 10 component skills of intelligence:
   The Basic Four: Relaxation, Attention, Motivation and Memory
   The Core Two: Communications and Computations
   The Higher Order Four: Concept Formation, Problem Solving, Creativity (mostly Accomplishment) and Precision Learning

All rest on a sub-framework of
  Modes: Inheritance, Trial-and-Error, Imitation and Instruction
  Conditions: Before, During and After
  Senses: Vision, Hearing, Smell, Taste, Touch, Intuition and Self-talk
  Tools: Action Plans, Practice and Reinforcement

6. And finally, this quote from Aristotle is to remind you to make the effort and take the time to build strong, productive, reliable habits:

We are what we repeatedly do.
Excellence, therefore, is not an act,
but a habit.
—Aristotle

Now, to get at the core of the work in this chapter, check out the sample Action Plans on the following pages.

SAMPLE ACTION PLAN

A. **OVERCOMING TEST ANXIETY**: (three weeks)

1. **Goal**: Be relaxed while studying well for a math test.

2. **Baseline**: Am relaxed three weeks before a test while not studying.

3. **Possible Steps**: (in imagination) (Review the Relaxation class first, and relax deeply before and during each of the following visualizations.)

   a. Looking at a math book.
   b. Reading one paragraph in math book.
   c. Doing one easy problem three weeks before test.
   d. Doing a problem two weeks before test.
   e. Doing a problem one week before test.
   f. Doing a problem three days before test.
   g. Doing a problem one day before test.
   h. Doing the first problem on the test.
   i. Completing the test.

(Remain deeply relaxed successfully at each step several times before moving to the next step. If unsuccessful, move back a step, and after experiencing success several times there, divide the next step into three or more smaller steps.)

4. **When, how often and how much**: 45 minutes, Monday, Wednesday and Friday, at 7 p.m. Conf-Level 7, continue for three weeks, then take a two-day break.

5. **Reinforcements**: Two raisins after each of the first three successes, then after every second success.

B. **DOUBLE READING SPEED & COMPREHENSION**: (three weeks)

Then,
C. Repeat A.
D. Repeat B.
E. Take one-week break.

Keep your goal in mind at all times. Let it drive you.

Now it's your turn — create your own sample action plan like the one below.

SAMPLE INITIAL ACTION PLAN FORM
An Exercise to Develop Precision Learning Skills

What I will do to increase my intelligence?
Fill this out quickly with your initial responses without thinking this first time. Then, later, you may modify them. The point is to let your brain circuits start their work on it.

How important to me is steadily increasing my ability to learn, to accomplish and to understand? (0 to 10) _____

How many minutes a day will I devote to it? _____

How many days a week? (circle) 1 2 3 4 5 6 7

Which day(s)? (circle) S M T W TH F S

At what time(s)? _____

On what date will I start? _____

Which skill will I start with?
_____

Which skill will I work with next?
_____

Where will I work on this?
_____

How clear am I about this (0 = fog to 10 = clear) _____

As I increase the levels of my learning skills, which personal goal(s) will I focus them on?
_____

How confident am I that I will follow this plan? (0-10)
_____

NAME: _____

DATE: _____

GETTING STARTED

Our main goal with this chapter is for you to sift, to begin to select from the information you've acquired, which of the component skills of intelligence to work on first. Pick just one skill to start.

This will be your first chunking effort.

When addressing the problem of how to make the most out of each of these chapters, I suggest using the "Tree." Draw a tree for each skill chapter using the main branches and twigs to identify the sections and their sub-ideas that are most important to you.

Review each tree from time to time to integrate that chapter into your understanding of the whole of intelligence. This chunking process allows you to focus your learning energies on what is most important to you at a particular time, yet at the same time absorbing an increasingly useful and active whole framework into your cognitive-emotional system.

BUILD THE SUCCESS HABIT

Take on a succession of simple, easy learning challenges and then when the success habit has become an integral part of you, a part of your muscles and bones, then take on slightly more difficult and complex learning challenges.

Above all, start. Risk making your first mistakes on your trip toward becoming an expert intelligence skill-builder.

> *Man's main task in life is to give birth to himself,*
> *to become what he potentially is.*
> *The most important product of his effort*
> *is his own personality.*
> —Erich Fromm

And finally, as you progress, consider this from an expert:

> *An expert is a person*
> *who has made all the mistakes*
> *that can be made in a very narrow field.*
> —Niels Bohr

CHAPTER THIRTEEN

SUMMARY:
THE BOOK IN A NUTSHELL

Intelligence is simply the ability to learn. It is expandable. Over the last 100 years, psychological researchers have increased our understanding of intelligence and its components so that it is becoming a skill, the kind of ability that is purposefully and infinitely improvable.

Skills are unique. The better you understand them, the more improvable they become. Because you use intelligence to improve itself, it is probably the most improvable of all skills. The better you understand intelligence and the more you improve it, the more power and skill you possess to improve it further.

For such a crucially important process, intelligence is relatively simple. In the Skilligence model of intelligence, there are four Learning Modes, three Learning Conditions and 10 Learning Processes.

You approach learning tasks along one or more of the four learning modes: Inheritance, Trial and Error, Imitation and Instruction. The three Conditions of learning are: Before, During and After.

When you learn about these Conditions, you can use them to maximize your learning progress by arranging them to reduce interference and distractions and to support and encourage the 10 Processes.

Relaxation is the most basic of the 10 Processes of intelligence. You must develop it to an adequate level before you can develop your Attention skill, and it before Motivation, and Motivation before Memory. All four of these basic skills are prerequisite to the two core Processes: Communications and Computations. And you must develop them to adequate levels before you succeed at developing the four higher-order Processes: Concept Formation, Problem Solving, Creativity and Precision Learning.

We are all born with the physiological substrate for each of these 10 Processes. We also develop each of them as abilities at home and in school as we mature. As we gain understanding of them, each also becomes a skill, improvable for as long as we live. As we learn about and improve them, our intelligence improves.

Like other skills, how much you actually increase your intelligence depends on: 1) how well you understand it and skill building in general; 2) how well you design your training program; 3) the amount of time and relaxed, energetic, intelligent and enjoyable effort you put into improving it. There is probably no limit to how much you can increase your intelligence.

Your intelligence is your most valuable possession. You use it to learn about, understand and accomplish everything that is important to you, including how to succeed in and enjoy your life.

The 10th process, Precision Learning, is the key to converting your intelligence into a skill. It is a magnificent set of six simple, user-friendly learning tools that can raise the probability of succeeding at a difficult learning task from below the 10 percent level to above the 90 percent level. Harness its power to assure your success improving the first nine Processes.

If you would like to begin taking advantage of this miracle of intelligence becoming a skill right before your eyes, first develop some familiarity and facility with the Precision Learning skill. Then use it to improve one of the other nine skills by a modest degree. Each time you understand and improve one skill a modest degree, you will increase your power to understand and improve the next. And the next....

Looking back a century from now, I believe that the most significant event of the 20th century will turn out to be — not the generation of nuclear explosions or power, nor the invention of the computer, but — the evolution of human intelligence into a skill.

To me, this is a miracle.

www.ingramcontent.com/pod-product-compliance
Lightning Source LLC
Chambersburg PA
CBHW031642040426
42453CB00006B/184